How Great Christians Met Christ

By
JAMES C. HEFLEY

MOODY PRESS
CHICAGO

© 1973 by
THE MOODY BIBLE INSTITUTE
OF CHICAGO

ISBN: 0-8024-0126-0

Printed in the United States of America

To

Mother and Dad

Acknowledgments

Appreciation is expressed to Harvest Publications of Chicago, Illinois, for permission to reprint the following copyrighted articles which appeared in *TODAY*: "The Case of the Skeptical Lawyer"; "When a Mission Cheated Lake Michigan"; "God's Grace for a Graceless Gob"; "A Tale of Two Brothers"; "Quest of the Gypsies"; "Billy Sunday Finds Home Base"; "The Parson Gets Converted" (here entitled "The Blacksmith's Advice"); "The Mountain Boy's Quest"; "The Shepherd's Dog"; and "The One-Eyed Apostle of Wales."

Appreciation is also expressed to David C. Cook Publishing Company for permission to reprint, "The Captain's Sword" which appeared in *SUNDAY DIGEST;* and to Union Gospel Press for permission to reprint, "Message from the Dying"; "The Prisoner's Joy"; and "The Curious Rabbi's Son," which were published in *GOSPEL HERALD.*

Contents

Introduction

The infant church of the first century rocked the mighty Roman Empire because men whose lives had been miraculously changed preached a miracle working gospel. For example, Paul had once been the chief persecutor of Christianity but was transformed by Christ into the chief preacher of the faith he once vowed to stamp out. It was he who declared, "If anyone is in Christ, he is a new creation. The old is gone. Look! the new has come" (2 Co 5:17, Berkeley).

As Paul and his comrades spread the miracle gospel throughout the world, the new came again and again as others experienced the transforming miracle of new birth in Christ. These converts carried the good news to others who, in turn, continued to spread the word. So it has been throughout almost twenty centuries as a miraculous chain has been forged that reaches to the space age.

This book contains the true stories of how forty-one of Christianity's greatest leaders were transformed miraculously. Before conversion, they were a motley crew—most of them hardly the type that could be expected to become spiritual leaders. But by God's grace, a foul-mouthed sailor became the author of "Amazing Grace"; an alcoholic became a preacher of hope; a famous athlete buried his life in China; and a mocker of ministers became a world-famous evangelist.

9

Here are the true stories of the conversions of such greats as Augustine, Luther, John Wesley, Newton, Spurgeon, Müller, Fuller, and Graham.

Their careers span almost twenty centuries; their experiences defy human understanding; their influence has been greater than that of kings and generals.

The Philosopher Who Searched for God

Justin Martyr

Justin, a young philosopher of the second century A.D., listened politely to the speech of another well-educated man.

"These people who follow the dead Nazarene are superstitious fools," the speaker said. "They worship nothing but clouds and the influence of the sky. I say they're a threat to the empire."

Heads nodded around the circle of men gathered there. But Justin was not so quick to agree. "I'm not so sure about that," he commented. "They are so sincere. I've heard of Christians who confessed their faith even though they knew they would be thrown into a caldron of boiling oil for their beliefs."

One of the men snickered. "Justin, you're not thinking of becoming a Christian, are you?"

"I want to know the truth," Justin answered soberly.

From his childhood Justin had been searching. He had inherited a sizable fortune which financed his travels throughout the Roman empire. He became a familiar traveler along the trade routes. Wherever he went in his search for knowledge and truth, he saw the persistent faith of the despised Christians.

11

"What is most important in life?" Justin asked a Stoic teacher. The Stoics believed that the world was God's body.

The man replied, "Seek for virtue."

A follower of Plato advised Justin to flee the world and in this way he would become like God by returning to the world of the pure spirit. But no matter how Justin tried, he could not suppress his bodily desires.

He received advice from other celebrated teachers, but none gave him an answer which satisfied. *Where, oh where,* he asked himself over and over, *is the meaning of life? Where is God, if there be a God?*

He thought again of the brave Christians he knew. At that time, Christianity was an illegal religion in the Roman empire. Thousands had died as martyrs. Justin had decided that the Christians were innocent of any real guile. He felt that they might possibly be misguided, but they certainly were not evil.

One day the seeking philosopher went for a walk in a lonely field near Ephesus. As he walked, he noticed that an old man was following behind him. Suddenly he turned and faced the stranger.

"Why are you staring at me?" the old man asked.

"I am surprised to find someone else in this quiet field," Justin replied.

"I am here to look for one of my household. But why are you here?" the old man queried.

"To exercise my reason."

"Does philosophy give one happiness?"

"Yes," Justin replied. But his tone was uncertain.

"Tell me, young man. What is philosophy and happiness?"

Justin gave a stock answer. "Philosophy is the full

knowledge of reality and the clear perception of truth. Happiness is the reward of such knowledge and wisdom."

"What is your definition of God?" the old man asked.

Again Justin used a glib answer from what he had been taught. "The changeless cause of all other things."

"Then can one know God without hearing one who has seen Him? How can the philosophers, who have never seen God, judge correctly?"

Justin answered by quoting Plato. "God can only be known by the mind, and then only when the mind is pure and well disposed."

The old man was not shaken. "There are ancient teachers who spake by the divine Spirit and foretold the future. They proved themselves by their predictions and miracles."

Justin stared quizzically at the old man. He could give no reply.

"Pray, my son, that the gates of light may be opened to you. These things can be understood only by the man to whom God and His Christ have given wisdom."

Justin never saw the old stranger again. Later he referred to the incident and wrote: "Straightway a flame was kindled in my soul and a love . . . of these men who are friends of Christ possessed me. I found this philosophy alone to be safe and profitable. Moreover, I wish that all . . . would not keep themselves away from . . . the Saviour."

When he came to believe that Christianity was the only true philosophy, Justin set out to tell other philosophers about Christ. After his baptism, he became a wandering teacher. He visited early Christian communities in such famous places as Ephesus, Alexandria, and Rome.

He took up his pen to challenge the critics and persecutors of Christianity. Today, almost 1800 years later, his *Apologies* are regarded as classics in Christian literature. Justin himself is looked upon as the greatest of the Christian apologists or defenders of the faith.

It was inevitable that Justin would clash with the Romans and be arrested for his teaching. In the year 163 A.D. he and several other Christians were brought before Rusticus, prefect of Rome. When Justin and his friends freely confessed their faith and refused to sacrifice to the pagan gods, they were beheaded.

After his death, the noted philosopher became known as Justin the Martyr. His noble example became an inspiration to future Christians who would die as martyrs because they chose to follow the despised Nazarene.

The Passionate Professor

Aurelius Augustine

"Sh, boy. Don't wake your mother. I don't want to hear one of her sermons."

Father and son quietly tiptoed into their Roman house, but she heard them in spite of their efforts. Monica had been hurt many times before by her husband who spent his nights in debauchery. Now she felt the hurt more deeply because her son Aurelius, who was barely seventeen, had accompanied his father in his revelry.

Aurelius looked at his tearful mother in pity, but said, "We had a good time." He was insensitive to her efforts to convert him to Christianity.

A year later Aurelius fathered an illegitimate child and shattered Monica by continuing to live with the child's mother for thirteen years without ever marrying her.

When his father died, Aurelius was well established in his life of immorality. Monica continued to pray for her son.

Aurelius became a professor and set up his own school in Carthage, North Africa. In those days most teaching was conducted in homes and rented halls, with tuition from the pupils paying the teacher's salary and other school expenses. His school, located on the Street of Bankers in the leading city of Africa, prospered. His pupils were the young blue bloods of the city. Someday, he mused, they would be government leaders. They would remember him with a choice appointment. Everything seemed to be fine.

Then Aurelius' school was destroyed by a marauding band. The frightening experience caused him to flee Africa. Next he set up a school in Rome where it seemed safer.

A pseudo-Christian group there, called the Manicheans, attracted the young professor. Aurelius became a zealous student of the cult that based its doctrines on a strange mixture of biblical and Greek philosophy. But he became disillusioned after talking to Bishop Faustus, a famous Manichean teacher. Aurelius decided that the man was nothing more than a cheap propagandist so he deserted the belief which he had held for nine years.

A year after arriving in Rome, the government appointed him professor of rhetoric in Milan. Aurelius invited his mother to join him. She had never stopped praying for his conversion.

In Milan, Aurelius was welcomed by Bishop Ambrose, a dedicated Christian leader and the city's most influential citizen. "Come hear me preach," the celebrated preacher invited.

Aurelius went indifferently to hear Bishop Ambrose. But the minister's polished way of speaking was so pleasing to Aurelius that he returned again and again. One day Ambrose preached about King David. "That David sinned is human, that he repented is exceptional," he said. "Men follow David into his sin; but they leave him when he rises into confession and repent-

16

ance." Aurelius' past immoral living rose to haunt him. Like David, he had sinned, but unlike David, he had not repented.

As feelings of personal guilt grew stronger, his doubts about Christianity began crumbling. Finally he could say sincerely that the Scriptures were inspired and that Jesus was the Son of God. Still his sinful passions led him to continue in his life of immorality.

His hungry heart wrestled with his sin until one day he entered a garden and threw himself under a fig tree, and cried, "O Lord, this hour make an end of my vileness."

That very moment he heard a child's voice outside the garden chanting, *"Tolle lege! Tolle lege! Take and read! Take and read!"*

Aurelius looked down. Before him was a copy of Romans, which he had left earlier. His eyes glanced upon the passage "Not in rioting and drunkenness, not in chambering and wantonness, not in strife and envying. But put ye on the Lord Jesus Christ, and make not provision for the flesh, to fulfill the lusts thereof" (Ro 13:13-14).

Joyously, Aurelius showed his close friend, Alypius, the passage. "I have put on Christ," he declared. "My heart is filled with peace."

Aurelius next hurried to tell his mother, Monica, that her long years of prayer had been answered. Then after special study, Aurelius was baptized by Bishop Ambrose.

Professor Aurelius Augustine spent forty-four fruitful years in the service of Christ during which he wrote seventy Christian books. One of his books, *The Confessions of St. Augustine*, has been ranked by

17

literary experts as one of the one hundred great books of all time. *The Confessions* are addressed to God and contain the frequently quoted phrase, "Thou hast made us for Thyself, and our heart is unquiet until it rests in Thee."

Augustine died peacefully in the year 430, shortly after Rome had fallen to the barbarians. He was then Bishop of Hippo in North Africa. When he died, the city was under siege by the Vandals from the North.

But his spiritual influence and teaching lived on through the Dark Ages, inspiring such Reformation leaders as Luther and Calvin to rebel against the hierarchy of corrupt Christendom.

Aurelius Augustine, the pagan professor who put on Christ in an Italian garden, is remembered today by many church historians as the most influential Christian since the time of the apostle Paul.

From Riches to Rags

Francis of Assisi

A merry-hearted laugh echoed through the stone prison. "That Francis," an inmate muttered. "One would think he was at a festival."

The other prisoner sighed. "But it's simple for him to stay happy. When peace is made between the cities, he'll be a free man."

Francesco Bernardrone, a twenty-year-old Italian of the early thirteenth century, had been captured in a war between his home city, Assisi, and its neighbor, Perugia. Imprisonment had cut short his dreams of knighthood.

But a year later, in November of 1203, Francis was free to return to the games, festivals, and parties, which his upper class set enjoyed. His friends gave him a resounding welcome, remembering that Francis, with his pranks and merry ways, had always been the life of the party.

A few weeks after his return home, however, Francis became gravely ill. One day after the crisis passed and he had regained some of his strength, he took a long walk into the open country. He should have enjoyed the fragrance of the spring flowers, but instead his conscience kept reminding him of his wasted youth.

Shortly thereafter, Francis was invited by a knight

to help fight a religious war. Thinking the excitement would take him out of the doldrums, Francis took up his shield and buckler and rode away. But on the road he became ill again, and the next day he came straggling back home.

During the days of recuperation, Francis thought more and more about his meaningless life. He noticed the crowds of beggars and poor people in the street outside his father's shop. To the chagrin of his tight-fisted merchant father, Francis tried to give purpose to his life by donating heavily to the poor.

One day after Francis had recovered, he was helping in his father's shop. A shabbily dressed beggar came in. "Something for me, young master? In God's name, please," he pleaded.

The impatient Francis hardly looked up. "Be gone," he shouted, and the beggar ran out into the street.

Suppose he had asked in the name of a baron," Francis thought when the man was gone. *I would have given him something. But he asked in the name of God and I chased him away.* Impulsively, Francis left the shop to find the beggar.

More and more the plight of the poor and the injustices in the life about him tugged at Francis' heart. Frequently he slipped away to a secluded cave. There he prayed, "Lord, show me the purpose of my life."

His father scolded him for his moodiness. His friends begged him to forget the poor and return to the social whirl. But Francis could not forget. He continued to pray.

One day in 1206, Francis was praying in a decaying old chapel outside the city. He felt that Christ spoke clearly to his heart.

"Lord Jesus, shed abroad Your light in the darkness of my mind," he whispered. "Be found of me, Lord, so that in all things I may act only in accordance with Thy holy will."

He paused to hear what he later declared was God's answer. "I have accepted you. Now I want your labor, your life, and all your being."

With a happy, new peace, Francis hurried home to tell his father that he had decided to sell all his belongings and become an apostle to the poor.

His merchant father was furious. When he saw that pleas and threats were of no avail, he disinherited Francis in a public ceremony. Francis tossed his remaining clothing and money to his father who took them and then callously turned his back on his son.

Francis left the city of Assisi clad only in an old mantle lent him by a gardener. During the next two years he stayed alive by begging and sleeping in the open. He spent his energies giving spiritual comfort to the poor and lepers and helping to rebuild crumbling churches.

In the year 1209, when Francis was only twenty-seven, a message came that set the course of the rest of his life. He believed that these words of Jesus in Matthew 10:8-10 were a direct commission to him: "Heal the sick, cleanse the lepers, raise the dead, cast out devils: freely ye have received, freely give. Provide neither gold, nor silver, nor brass in your purses, nor scrip for your journey, neither two coats, neither shoes, nor yet staves: for the workman is worthy of his meat."

The words convinced Francis that he was on the right road. He discarded his shoes and purse and began gathering a band of companions who agreed with him to live by the rule of the biblical commission. The brothers, as they called themselves, went out two by two on their gospel tours. They sang, preached, and distributed food and clothing to the needy in the city squares and marketplaces.

Upon entering the order, the brothers sold all their material possessions and gave the receipts to the poor and needy. They were expected to continue their trade, or learn one if they had none, and give their earnings to the poor.

The people easily noticed the difference between the poor brothers and the selfish church leaders who gloried in wealth. They took notice of the morally clean lives which the brothers lived while some leading clergymen made jokes about their scandalous sins.

The work of Francis and his brothers came as a fresh breath of revival during the Dark Ages. And, although he lived only seventeen years as the apostle to the poor, his example is an inspiration today to Christians of all denominations. This man who lived three centuries before Luther is called by Protestant church historian Phillip Schaff, "one of the spiritual lights of the Dark Ages."

The Mountain Boy's Quest

Ulrich Zwingli

Seven-year-old Ulrich Zwingli dangled his feet from an Alpine ledge, while his brothers herded the flock together. He gazed across the snow-topped mountains toward Zurich, not dreaming of the part he would play in the city's future.

"Let's go, loafer. The sun is sinking fast," one of his brothers called from below.

"Let me admire the work of God a little longer," he pleaded.

"Time enough for that at mass."

Ulrich sighed as he picked up the short shepherd's staff his father had whittled for him. He thought of the monotonous Latin chanting of the village priest, which none of the people understood. As he followed his brothers reluctantly down the narrow path, he murmured aloud, "I can see more of God here than I can in church."

The following year, Ulrich's father sent him to study with an uncle who was a priest. Two years later, he was sent to a private school at Basel, Switzerland, where he studied Greek and Latin.

By his thirteenth birthday his interests included music, writing, and poetry. The Dominican monks saw the budding young genius and begged him to enter the monastery.

"I'm not so sure that's what God wants me to do," the precocious boy replied. "How can I find God while I'm shut up in a castle?"

An urgent message from his father advised, "Come home at once. Don't let the monks influence you."

Ulrich's father was beginning to question the teachings of Rome, so instead of entering the monastery, Ulrich went to study at the University of Vienna. He enjoyed his classical studies there, but he complained that he was learning too much about heathen poets and not enough about Christ.

In the year 1507, he received his doctorate. He was only twenty-two. Still he wanted to acquire more religious knowledge.

"Thomas Wyttenback can teach you the Scriptures," a student friend assured him.

Wyttenback turned out to be a bold reformer. He showed Ulrich how purgatory, prayers to the saints, and the rule of the priests were not in agreement with the Bible.

"But if I can't trust the church, whom can I trust?" Ulrich wailed.

"You can trust Christ," his teacher retorted. "He alone bore your sins, not the priests."

Ulrich Zwingli studied his Latin Bible late into the night. When he returned to the teacher, his convictions were shaped. "I have put my trust in Christ for the forgiveness of my sins," he declared.

It was obvious how much this decision meant in the years ahead. After further studies, Ulrich Zwingli boldly stepped out in opposition to the Roman church.

In 1520, while serving as pastor in Zurich, he proclaimed, "The Word of God will take its course as surely as does the Rhine; one may dam it up for awhile but cannot stop its flow."

The Word of God did take its course. Across the Alps in Germany, Luther took his stand, not unaware of Zwingli's impassioned preaching. Thirteen years later, John Calvin made known his convictions on justification by faith. Two years after that, Menno Simons joined the ranks of the Reformers. Then came John Knox, the Scottish firebrand, his convictions also tempered by the writings of Zwingli.

These five—Zwingli, Luther, Calvin, Menno Simons, and Knox—shook all of Europe during the sixteenth century. But the mountain boy, Ulrich Zwingli, who became the Reformer of Switzerland, was the first among them to trust wholly in Christ.

Light for the Blind Monk

Martin Luther

"*Mea culpa; mea culpa*—my sins, my sins," the young monk cried, as he threw himself on the floor before his superior.

"Give me God's mercy and yours," he begged.

"Poverty, chastity, and obedience must be your dearest companions," the prior intoned.

Young Martin Luther, son of a German peasant, took his solemn vows. Then clad in a woolen undergarment, black gown, short cowl, and black belt, he started out to earn God's mercy.

And how hard he tried. He fasted for days at a time. He cast off his blankets at night and almost froze while doing penance. He lay prostrate on the floor and moaned his prayers.

Later he wrote, "If ever a monk got to heaven by the monkery route I would have gotten there. . . . I should have martyred myself, if I had kept it up longer with watching, praying, reading, and other labors."

Dr. John Staupitz, the vicar-general of the Augustinian order to which Luther belonged, tried to help. "Christ is the forgiveness of sins," he told the young monk. "But you must have a catalogue with real sins written in it if He is to help you."

Luther tried naming his sins, but this did not bring peace. He pored over a red leather Latin Bible, searching for relief from his burden.

One day in 1508, he was sitting in his tiny tower cell reading the book of Romans. When he came to the seventeenth verse of the first chapter, his first flash of light came. "The just shall live by faith." He rolled the sentence over and over in his mind. Was faith alone enough? He wondered.

Then he received word from his superior that he and another monk had been selected to visit Rome to appeal for a reform among the Augustinian monks. Luther's heart leaped when he heard the news. Surely in the holy city he would find the spiritual peace his heart craved.

When Luther's eyes first gazed upon the city, he fell on his face, crying, "Hail, holy Rome."

He visited every shrine he could find in the city, seeking indulgences for his sins. He came to the famed Sancta Sanctorum, in which was a flight of twenty-eight steps, reputed to be the very steps which Christ climbed in Pilate's judgment hall. Luther knew that Pope Leo IV had promised an indulgence of nine years for each step climbed by a pilgrim on his knees while saying the designated prayers.

As he inched his way up the worn stairs, Luther's voice intoned the prayers. In between prayers he confessed every sin he could bring to mind.

Suddenly he recalled the portion of Scripture he had once read in his tower cell. "The just shall live by faith." The truth shook his inner being. He hesitated for a moment, then abruptly got to his feet and descended the stairs.

The light was dawning, but spiritual darkness still gripped his soul.

Back in Germany, Luther searched the Scriptures still further. He meditated for hours in Psalms, Romans, and Galatians.

In a solemn ceremony, the University of Wittenberg granted him the degree of doctor of theology. This entitled him to teach theology. But, as he wrote later, "When I was made Doctor, I did not yet know the light."

He lectured on the Psalms, then pushed on into Romans where he wrestled anew with the doctrine of justification by faith. He hated the phrase, "the righteousness of God," because he believed that was the attribute which God used to punish sinners. Still he came back to the sentence, "The just shall live by faith."

Soon the light burst forth and illumined every corner of his dark heart. Later he said, "I saw that the righteousness of God is received from God by faith as a gift. I saw that this was the means by which the merciful God declares the believers righteous."

"I felt myself new-born. All the Scriptures appeared different to me. Instead of hating, now I intensely loved God's righteousness."

And so the new Luther was born—the Luther who set all Europe afire with his preaching of justification by faith.

The Priest and the Hedge Preachers

Menno Simons

The bearded Dutch priest eyed the knot of farmers gathered around a stall in the village market. He noticed the wooden staves at their belts. *What a contrast to the men of my parish who wear sharp swords,* he thought.

Slyly he sought information about the Anabaptists, or "hedge preachers" as they were called. "They refuse to have their children baptized," a fellow cleric told him. "They perform their own marriage ceremonies and have their own worship."

Menno Simon's beard bobbed up and down. "I see. I see. They are like the Lutheran heretics."

"In some ways, Father, but unlike the followers of Luther they do not court the favor of princes. They believe church and state should be strictly separate."

"They should be arrested," the Dutch priest thundered.

"Nay, but Father, they are too honest to be charged by the law. They have many friends in the village— many Catholics. Besides they are fleet of foot when in danger of persecution."

I am a new priest here, Menno Simons mused. *If I*

29

should cause them to be arrested, the people might turn on me. He looked away as if in deep thought. *Hmm. I know. I shall engage these hedge heretics in debate. I shall show them up before the village.*

"Why do you refuse to let the one true church baptize your children?" Menno Simons bombarded them with questions. "Why do you set up ceremonies of your own? Who is your pope?"

The Anabaptist leader with whom he was debating replied softly. "We conduct our lives and our worship only by Scripture," he said. "We desire only to be left alone. We are not troublemakers."

"Only by Scripture," Menno Simons continued with a sneer. "What part do you give holy tradition? And who gave you hedge preachers the authority to interpret Scripture?"

The gentle hedge preacher was not to be taunted into anger. "We abide only by Scripture," he repeated and then remained silent.

"All right All right!" the bearded Menno shouted back. "I will prove you are heretics—by Scripture. We will meet again."

The Anabaptist nodded soberly. "We shall pray that God will open your eyes—through Scripture," he said as he turned away.

For the first time in his priestly life, Menno Simons began to study the New Testament seriously. And, unknown to his superiors, he began reading the writings of Luther. At first he tried to put aside his doubts by telling himself, "It is the devil trying to lure me away from the true faith."

But disturbing thoughts kept invading his mind. While he was saying Mass he found himself thinking,

I cannot possibly turn this bit of bread into the flesh of Christ.

Shaken, Menno Simons took his doubts to his superior. The cleric smiled. "Father, there are some things we do which are not directly based upon Scripture. But the councils and sacred tradition give us ample authority."

Menno went away without relief. He paid closer attention to the simple Anabaptists. He noticed that they baptized only believers. He heard stories of their honesty, purity, and thriftiness.

Then a most disturbing event occurred. His brother became an Anabaptist. At the same time, the persecution of the hedge preachers became more intense. Menno feared for his brother's life.

Then in the year 1535, a dusty messenger ran into Menno's residence. He reported that three hundred Anabaptists had been slaughtered by civil soldiers while hiding in an old monastery. Menno was aghast at the news. "They did not resist?" he asked.

The messenger solemnly shook his head. "All were killed except the women and children. Even your brother."

"My brother!" Menno's voice was breaking, as he waved the messenger away.

Menno spent long hours in meditation and prayer. Then he visited his superior and resigned his office as a village priest.

When he began preaching his new beliefs, his old colleagues in the church vigorously denounced him. Soldiers chased him out of the area to the province of Gronigen. Shortly afterward he was baptized and ordained an elder among the Anabaptists. Soon he became the most famous hedge preacher of all. In 1542, the Emperor Charles V commanded, "On penalty of death no one is to receive Menno Simons into his house or on his property. No one is to speak with him, give him shelter, provision, or read his books."

Menno fled to Cologne, Germany, where a tolerant ruler let him preach and write in peace. For seventeen more years Menno led a fruitful life, writing and preaching to all who would listen. He died on January 31, 1561.

Today, Menno is remembered for the doctrine of religious liberty which he fostered. Almost four hundred thousand Mennonites, named after the renowned hedge preacher,—along with other free-church members—salute the bearded Reformer as a champion of the open Bible and the truth that sets men free.

The Minister's Mimic

George Whitefield

"My beloved brethren and sisters. Give ear to the words of my mouth. I speak the message of the Almighty."

The crowd at the bar roared with laughter. "Bravo, lad! Bravo," a stocky man shouted as he lifted his glass of brew.

"If I couldn't see you, boy, I'd be scared out of my wits," another customer said. "To think of old Preacher Cole thundering forth in your mother's tavern."

Young George Whitefield, barely fifteen, was up to his favorite trick of mimicking Mr. Cole, the pastor of the Southgate Chapel in Gloucester, England. Mimicking the neighborhood minister had become a nightly amusement for him while he tended the bar for his mother and step-father.

George Whitefield's talent for mimicking and dramatic acting was well known in the neighborhood. At school he was always called upon to bring the speech when the mayor paid his annual visit. Sometimes he was truant from school for days at a time to practice parts in dramatic plays.

When he reached fifteen, his schooling ended. His mother said he was needed to help out in the family tavern. So the youth who would one day become a world-famous evangelist spent the afternoons and evenings mopping the floor, serving brew, and mimicking Mr. Cole, the minister.

One night, George and his cronies even broke in on a service conducted by the minister. Shouting "Old Cole! Old Cole!" the boys almost turned the meeting into pandemonium.

What George's friends and the tavern customers did not know was that underneath George was really interested in Mr. Cole's sermons. Often after the tavern had closed, the youth sat up late reading the Bible.

One day a friend came by the tavern to suggest that George think of going to Oxford. "You can work your way through," the friend said.

George consulted with his mother, and it was agreed that he should return to grammar school and finish his studies to qualify for the university.

When the young bartender finally reached Oxford, he met John and Charles Wesley. The brothers had formed the Holy Club called by mocking students "The Godly Club," "Bible Moths," "Bible Bigots," and most frequently, "Methodists" because of the regular routine of worship which they followed.

But George was attracted by the strict religious and devotional habits which the Wesley brothers observed. In his second year at Oxford he joined the club, vowing to live by the rule.

He fasted and prayed as religiously as the other Holy Club members. But to his disappointment, he found no soul peace.

Charles Wesley lent him a book called *The Life of God in the Soul of Man*. The teachings of the book shone into young Whitefield's heart like rays of light. "God showed me," Whitefield wrote later, "that true religion was union of the soul with God, and Christ proved within us."

Seeking this true religion, George Whitefield gave himself to incessant prayer. Night after night he groaned and agonized on his bed, bidding Satan to depart from him. He tried living on a starvation diet and giving almost all of his money to the poor. He wore coarse woolen gloves, a patched gown, and dirty shoes. Finally, his feverish seeking for union with God made him ill.

Then one day he remembered that Jesus' declaration of His thirst had come when He hung on the cross. His sufferings were almost finished. Young Whitefield suddenly threw himself down on his bed. "I thirst! I thirst!" he cried.

Later he testified of what happened. "Soon after this, I felt in myself that I was delivered from the burden. The spirit of mourning was taken from me, and I knew what it was to truly rejoice in God my Saviour."

Barely a year later, Whitefield was preaching his "new birth" doctrine in London's largest churches. All England soon became excited over the boy preacher with the golden voice.

At the invitation of the Wesley brothers, Whitefield went to America. He led a dramatic spiritual awakening in Georgia. Returning to England, he found he was more popular than ever. When the embarrassed state church locked its doors to him, Whitefield took to the fields and preached to crowds of thirty thousand and more. Large numbers of his hearers professed experiencing the new birth.

Back to America he went. His ministry was so fruitful that even skeptical Benjamin Franklin declared, "It seems as if all the world is growing religious." George Whitefield was then only twenty-six years old.

For thirty more years Whitefield preached to large crowds, shuttling back and forth across the Atlantic. He died in 1770, still praying for those who would not heed the call of Christ. Lord Bolingbroke, the skeptic, called him "the most extraordinary man in our times."

Mercy for the Missionary

John Wesley

The ship lurched crazily as it inched its way through twenty-foot-high waves in the Atlantic. A wall of water burst across the deck, split the mainsail of the eighteenth-century sailing vessel, and sloshed into the living quarters.

The Reverend John Wesley shuddered in fear. Several Englishmen around him screamed. But when he glanced at a group of Moravians, he marveled that they were calmly singing a psalm. "Heavy-minded and dull-witted folk," he thought.

When the seas had calmed, Wesley edged up to their leader. "Were you not afraid in the storm?" he inquired.

"No. The Lord is on our side. We do not fear death."

The next day the Moravian pastor, Spangenberg, had a question for the English minister. "Friend Wesley, do you know Jesus Christ?" he inquired.

"I know that He is the Saviour of the world," the dignified Englishman replied blandly.

"But can you tell me if He has saved you?"

Wesley was plainly flustered. "I hope so," he answered uneasily.

John Wesley was on his way to Georgia to evangelize the Indians. But before he was to find peace in the faith of the Moravians, he was to wail, "I came to Georgia to convert the Indians, but oh, who shall convert me? I have but a fair summer religion."

Although Wesley was an Oxford graduate and sternly religious his "fair summer religion" failed to move the indifferent English colonists, much less the pagan Indians. He returned to England after two years, his missionary journey a failure.

He discovered that all over England people were talking about the preaching of his former classmate at Oxford, George Whitefield. Whitefield had had a dramatic conversion experience and was preaching the new birth to large audiences.

At this time, John Wesley's brother, Charles, fell ill. John hurried to his bedside, only to find that Peter Bohler, a Moravian, had arrived first. Peter Bohler was plying the sick man with questions about his faith.

John wrote later in his *Journal* that he heard enough of the conversation to "convince me of my want of faith."

He felt that he should no longer preach. But Bohler advised him to tell others the truth until he had it himself.

Two days later, John Wesley told a condemned prisoner that he could have his sins forgiven by simply trusting in Christ. "I will," the prisoner said. "Now, I am fully prepared to die," he added with deep feeling. "Christ has taken away my sins." The prisoner had full assurance, but poor Wesley struggled on.

On May 20, 1738, Charles Wesley received the full assurance of his salvation after reading Luther's *Commentary on Galatians*.

About five A.M. on the following Wednesday, John opened his Testament to 2 Peter 1:4 and read, "Whereby are given unto us exceeding great and precious promises: that by these ye might be partakers of the divine nature."

That evening he was invited to a Christian society meeting in Aldersgate Street. "I went very unwillingly," he later wrote in his journal, "to hear one who was reading Luther's preface to Romans."

That was to be his victory night. Here is how he described it: "About a quarter before nine, while he was describing the change which God works in the heart through faith in Christ, I felt my heart strangely warmed . . . I felt I did trust in Christ alone for salvation."

He could scarcely wait to tell Charles. Bursting into his room, he shouted, "I believe."

"Let us sing a hymn together, brother," Charles suggested.

John agreed, and the two sang a new hymn which Charles had written only the day before—a song still sung by Christians today, "Christ the Friend of Sinners."

> Where shall my wondering soul begin!
>   How shall I to heaven aspire?
> A slave redeemed from death and sin.
>   A brand plucked from eternal fire.
> How shall I equal triumphs raise,
>   Or sing my great Deliverer's praise?

Eighteen days later, John Wesley preached at the University of Oxford a long-remembered sermon, "By grace are ye saved through faith." This sounded the keynote of a ministry during which he is credited with saving England from moral anarchy, winning tens of thousands to Christ, and founding the Methodist church.

God's Grace for a Graceless Gob

John Newton

Struggling against the strong waves and floating debris, John Newton fought his way up to the *Greyhound's* deck. There he helped put the pumps into action and joined the crew in frantically bailing water and stopping leaks.

By nine A.M. the leaks were crammed with bedding and clothes, held in place by the planks which had been nailed over them. The sea was running high, the leaky ship rocking crazily. The crew had to lash themselves to the deck to keep from being swept overboard.

John Newton's body was aching with exhaustion. Almost without thinking he muttered, "Lord, have mercy on us." Instantly his numbed brain jolted awake. He had not prayed since childhood. Would God—if He existed at all, and John Newton doubted that He did—have mercy on such a blasphemer?

Although seamen on British trading ships were not known for their piety, the ship's captain had only a few days before begged Newton to cease his blood-curdling blasphemies. Newton's epithets were not the common swearings of a hearty sailor. His curses expressed his revulsion against the very idea of God.

After his surprising utterance, the ship's star blasphemer left the pumps to relieve the captain at the

41

helm. Every time the ship lurched into a dark trough of boiling water, Newton feared they could not possibly escape death. But the angry Atlantic finally leveled off, and he went below to collapse in his bunk.

When he took up steering duties again, Newton noticed that most of the ship's sails had blown away. The wind was blowing through bare spars, making navigation almost impossible.

Seven days passed, and no land was in sight. Food supplies shrank to a handful of salted codfish. One man died. The worried captain called his crew together. Eying Newton, he said, "Ye men know I picked this fellow up on the African coast to take him home to his father. I grant ye he knows how to navigate, because he once skippered his own slave ship. But since he's been my assistant we've had nothing but trouble, trouble, trouble."

"Aye, Cap'n, ye speak the truth," a scar-faced deck hand cried.

"He says he's a freethinker. I know his father never taught him this way. His blasphemies are enough to make the sea cough up her dead. Like Jonah in the Bible, I think he's a curse to us."

John Newton flexed his strapping muscles and stepped back as the crew glared at him accusingly. They wouldn't throw him overboard. Or would they? He glared back at the captain.

"We'll wait," the old trader finally said. "But John Newton, ye'd better join us in prayer if ye value your hide."

Newton strode silently back to his post. A verse of Scripture he'd heard as a child came to his mind. "If ye then, being evil, know how to give good gifts unto your children; how much more shall your heavenly Father give the Holy Spirit to them that ask him?" (Luke 11:13).

"God, if You're true," he prayed between clenched teeth, "You'll make good your word. Cleanse Thou my vile heart."

Four weeks later, in the month of April 1748, the *Greyhound* limped into an Irish harbor. Newton went to church and there professed salvation.

The blasphemous freethinker became a powerful evangelical preacher. His testimony found expression in sacred poetry. The poem that best expresses his redemption is a beloved hymn still sung by Christians today.

> Amazing grace! How sweet the sound
> That saved a wretch like me!
> I once was lost but now am found,
> Was blind, but now I see.

The One-Eyed Apostle of Wales

Christmas Evans

"Born on Christmas Day!" the peasant father exclaimed. "Aye, we don't have much to give him but a name. And what'll that be, lassie?"

Joanna Evans' eyes turned tenderly toward the infant snuggling beside her. "We'll name him Christmas because that's his birthday," she said simply.

And so was born in the year 1766, the boy later to be known as the apostle of wild Wales.

In his early years, Christmas Evans experienced many unpleasant situations and near-tragedies. After his father died, he lived with his cruel uncle. Then he farmed himself out as servant to whoever would feed him. He was stabbed in a quarrel. He was rescued from drowning. He fell from a high tree with an open knife in his hand. A horse he was riding ran away, dashing through a low, narrow passage.

At eighteen he could not read a word. But he knew that he was a sinner and that but for the providence of God he would be in hell. When a spiritual revival flamed up among the youth of Cardiganshire, the homeless boy sought refuge in Christ.

"I must read the Bible," he told the Welsh villagers at the Arminian Presbyterian church he attended.

"That's good, Christmas," they told him. "But, lad, not one in seven in these parts can even spot a letter."

A few months later, Christmas Evans amazed his acquaintances by stumbling through a Scripture passage. Then he set more tongues to wagging by announcing, "God has called me to preach."

He sought out his pastor for help. "Sir, will you teach me?" he stammered, the light of learning brightened his craggy features.

The minister agreed, and so he taught young Christmas for six months. Then, his funds running low, the youth decided to journey to England. "I'll work in the harvest, then return for more schooling," he told his teacher.

On the road he was overtaken by a mob. They beat him fiercely leaving him bruised and sightless in one eye.

But Christmas Evans did not give up. He came home and studied harder, mastering Greek, Hebrew, and Latin. He threw himself into a wearisome itinerant ministry that carried him by horse and gig along thousands of miles of rugged trails, and earned himself the name Apostle of Wales. Thousands were converted and many new churches established through his ministry.

The Case of the Curious Cobbler

William Carey

To a passing stranger, it looked like an ordinary English shoe shop. There was the customary shingle out front, "Secondhand shoes bought and sold." But local people in the village of Paulers Pury knew that the young apprentice there was not an ordinary cobbler.

They called him "Columbus" because he spoke so often of the great discoverer. They laughed at him when he studied foreign languages at night. "Why do you need to learn so many languages, Columbus?" they taunted.

The youth replied meekly, "I would like to understand men of other nations."

William Carey was stirred by the reports of explorers who had followed Columbus. He kept a map on the wall, and as new information became available, he carefully classified it on the map.

He read every book he could get his hands on, even copies of old sermons. One day he was reading from the famous divine, Jeremy Taylor. He became disturbed and spoke to an apprentice friend whom he knew was a regular churchgoer.

"What's this business about being born again?"

Carey asked. "I was baptized into the Church of England, but I've never heard of this."

His friend, William Warr, spoke up quickly. "Being baptized is not enough. Now take the Dissenters Church which I attend. My preacher will tell you how to be sure that you're right with God."

"But the Dissenters are heretics," Carey argued.

"They may be called heretics, friend Carey," William Warr countered, "but they preach from the Bible. And that's what counts."

Carey argued with his friend for several months before finally giving in and attending a Dissenters service. After going a few times, he had to admit that the Dissenters did indeed preach from the Book. "I'll go to church three times on Sunday and stop my lying and swearing," he resolved.

Then England was suddenly plunged into a war with France and Spain. The enemy's fleet moved into the Channel and threatened invasion. King George proclaimed February 10, 1779, to be a national day of fasting and prayer. That day Carey joined the Dissenters in a special service.

The minister, Thomas Chater, led the group in prayer; then he talked about the reproach of following Christ. Carey reported later, "I felt ruined and helpless. I had a desire to follow Christ."

And follow Christ He did! After his new birth Carey couldn't learn enough about the Bible. He began studying Greek and Hebrew, and during morning devotions he read a portion of the Bible in three languages—Hebrew, Greek, and Latin.

After his master died, Carey opened his own cobbler's shop. He married and started a night school for village children. He used a crude leather globe to show the children where explorers had traveled; and often after his students had left, he sat far into the night with Bible in hand, as he meditated upon the pagan millions in other lands. On his wall map he scribbled in all he knew about the religion of every nation.

On August 10, 1786, the zealous cobbler was ordained to the Baptist ministry. A few weeks afterward he was attending a minister's meeting at Northhampton. One of the older ministers suggested that someone name a topic for general discussion. Carey arose and posed the question of "whether or not the Great Commission is binding upon us today to go and teach all nations."

The circle of ministers grew quiet. Then the moderator looked severely at Carey. "Sit down, young man. When God pleases to convert the heathen, He will do it without your aid or mine." But Carey was not to be silenced so easily.

On May 30, 1792, he delivered a history-making sermon at the Baptist Minister's Association in Nottingham. He made two memorable declarations: "Expect great things from God. Attempt great things for God." The next morning he proposed forming a missionary society. Four months later the society was formed with capital less than a hundred dollars. The following year, Carey and his family sailed for India as missionaries of the new society.

There followed for the indomitable Carey a long and illustrious missionary career that was often marred by tragedy. His wife and a fellow missionary became mentally unbalanced and had to be placed in an institution. Other missionaries succumbed to Oriental diseases. It was seven years before Carey baptized his first convert.

Yet during his missionary career, the cobbler who believed in expecting great things from God and attempting great things for God translated the entire Bible into the four leading languages of India and made the Bible available to three hundred million people in their own language. Besides this, he was the key figure in setting up 126 mission schools.

Even more important, he triggered missionary movements in England and America. Today Carey is rightfully called the father and forerunner of the modern missionary movement.

When he was dying, the great missionary pioneer whispered, "When I am gone, say nothing about Dr. Carey. Speak about Dr. Carey's Saviour."

The Blacksmith's Advice

Francis Asbury

Fourteen-year-old Francis walked around the huge forge that was puffing and spouting fire.

"Big one isn't she, my boy?" the tall blacksmith said pridefully. "There's not another like it in the valley. But now to your duties."

In no time at all, Francis Asbury developed a strong liking for the broad-shouldered, hulking Mr. Foxall. It was a good thing, for he had six more years of apprenticeship ahead.

"You a Christian lad, my boy?" the blacksmith asked him one day as they were shoveling coal together.

Francis laughed merrily. "I suppose so. At school they called me the Parson. I go to church every Sunday, and I can't remember ever telling a lie or cursing."

"That isn't what I mean, Francis. A Christian is one who has a personal relationship with Christ the Saviour. Now take what happened to me for instance," the blacksmith said. Then he put his shovel aside and told young Francis the story of his conversion. When he finished, the boy was staring solemnly into the coal bin.

"Strange, I've never heard my minister talk like that," he said.

"Maybe he doesn't preach the gospel," the blacksmith suggested. "Now take the West Bromwich church. Some of the greatest ministers in England preach there. Why don't you visit there?"

Francis did. He also went to the church in Wednesbury, where not many years before, a mob threatened Charles Wesley.

"The services are so different," he told his mother. "The preachers have no prayer books, yet they pray wonderfully. The people sing hymns and during the sermon often shout "Amen." If they did that in our church, our pastor's wig would fall off." Francis chuckled at the thought.

Francis kept attending the evangelical services. He began earnestly to seek the forgiveness of his sins.

Then he heard one minister, a Mr. Mather, say, "A real believer is as happy as if he was in heaven."

Francis' hopes fell. "Will I ever be that happy?" he moaned to himself.

He continued in a distressed condition until a weekday prayer meeting at Wednesbury. The minister declared, "The only qualification you need to come to Christ is to know that you're sinful and helpless."

"I have those qualifications," Francis assured himself.

"The rest is up to you," the minister continued. "You have only to believe and come."

Francis fled to his father's barn and fell on his knees. There he found refuge in Christ.

Right away he gave expression to his faith. First he became a class leader, then a local preacher.

In 1771, John Wesley's preachers met in Bristol for their annual conference. In the conference Wesley pleaded, "Our brethren in America call for help. Who will go?"

"I will," shouted Francis Asbury, as he sprang to his feet. He was only twenty-six at the time.

In the colonies, the muscles he had tempered in the blacksmith's shop served him well. For thirty-three years he averaged riding six thousand miles each year. He preached seventeen thousand sermons and was made a Methodist bishop charged with the administration of all the Methodist churches in America. During his ministry, Methodists led all other American denominations in evangelistic zeal. When Asbury came to America, Methodists ranked numerically in last place. Barely a few years after his death, Methodists were declared the leading denomination in the New World.

Salvation for a Scholar

Henry Martyn

The plain-faced little boy with warts on his hands peered through the crowd at the aging John Wesley. He was only eight, but he could feel the brittle tenseness in the crowd. On one side of Mr. Wesley was a multitude of laboring men who had been clamoring for a raise in wages. On the other side was a squad of the Crown's soldiers sent to keep order.

How much young Henry Martyn absorbed from John Wesley's gospel of peace we do not know. But we do know that the future Apostle to Persia grew up in the world of the Wesleys.

At school, Henry did not behave as Methodist doctrine said he should. His irritability caused the older boys to bully and tease him, and when they did, he flew into a violent rage. But he survived the bullies and in 1797, when he was seventeen, he took the coach from his home in Truro village to Cambridge.

At the university, Henry Martyn was much more interested in making the top examinaton grades of his class than he was in the dry preaching he heard daily at the five-thirty chapel. But there was sister Sally to be reckoned with. Back home she prayed regularly for her scholarly big brother.

After two years at Cambridge, Henry had reached his goal and stood first in his class. His father's eyes sparkled with pride upon hearing the news.

But Sally was not so glad. "Knowing the Bible is more important than knowing the mathematical theorems of Euclid," she attested.

Henry came back with a scalding remark that caused Sally to choke back the tears. But at her next opportunity she reminded him again that he should read the Bible. Reluctantly he consented.

Henry stayed at the university during the Christmas holidays of 1799. He was not eager to have Sally ask him about his promise to read the Scriptures.

The news of his father's sudden and unexpected death, coming during the holidays on January 1, jolted him to reality as Sally's reminders had not been able to do.

"I began to consider that invisible world to which my father had gone," he wrote later. "I had no taste for studies and took up my Bible, thinking that this solemn time was suitable for consideration of religion."

The young Cambridge scholar began studying the doctrines of the apostles. He added daily prayer and solemn meditation upon Doddridge's *Rise and Progress of Religion in the Soul*. But doctrine and prayer did not lead him to a satisfying faith.

Finally he turned to the gospels. There he heard the voice of Christ making offers of mercy and forgiveness. "I began to devour them with delight," he testified. "My heart responded, and I began praying with eagerness and hope."

There came no emotion-packed moment of dramatic conversion, but four years later he could say, "The

54

Word is real. The whole current of my desires is altered. I am walking quite another way."

In 1805—barely five years after his father's death—Henry Martyn sailed for India as chaplain for the East India Company. Meditation upon the state of the lost heathen, and upon the *Journal* of the saintly David Brainerd had driven him to dedicate his life to missionary service. He left behind the girl he loved because of her poor health and abandoned the opportunity of possibly becoming one of England's greatest pulpiteers.

A year after he reached Calcutta, Martyn began translating the New Testament into Hindustani. In addition, he started supervising translations into Persian and Arabic.

Henry Martyn gave only six short years to missionary work. His greatest desire was to take a Persian New Testament to the Persians. Although suffering with advanced tuberculosis, he gave the last year of his life to negotiating with Persian leaders. His last two months were spent in making a torturous journey to give his Persian Testament to the British ambassador, who in turn gave it to the Shah of Persia.

But though he was buried beneath Persian sands, Henry Martyn's dedication has lived on. His burning devotion to Christ and his compassion for pagan people have sent multitudes of youth to the mission field. Today, his letters and diary are still counted among the most treasured records of Christian discipleship.

A Tale of Two Brothers

Robert McCheyne

Once there were two Scottish brothers, David and Robert.

David was so sensitive to truth that whenever he heard the slightest exaggeration, a shadow would flit across his face. He was scholarly and quiet and spent most of his leisure time helping the younger members of his family.

David was a devoted Christian. Too devoted, his younger brother, Robert, often thought. Especially when he came home from an evening of dancing and found David in earnest prayer.

"Really, Dave," he said once after tiptoeing in and finding the older boy kneeling. "I heard you call my name. Am I that bad?"

David tried to explain. "We're all sinners in God's sight, Bob. I'm praying that you'll trust in Christ instead of yourself."

Robert enrolled in the University of Edinburgh. He won award after award in the languages, drawing, music, and poetry.

"You have most remarkable talents," his philosophy professor told him. "Develop them to the fullest."

At home David grew weak and sickly. But his prayers for Robert at the university were as fervent as ever. His illness stretched out into long months. Only the light of his faith kept his spirits bright. And still he prayed for Robert.

Robert was eighteen when David died peacefully. With eyes red rimmed and swollen from weeping, Robert sought comfort in his brother's Saviour. From the day of David's death, the first streaks of spiritual dawn showed in his heart. His poetry blossomed into hymns of faith. His brilliant mind centered upon the Scriptures. Less than a year after his brother's death, he entered the Divinity College at Edinburgh.

The young brother moved on to become the most popular Presbyterian minister in Scotland and the British Isles. At twenty-three he became pastor of St. Peter's Church of Dundee, where his flock numbered over four thousand.

Robert's ministry lasted only seven years, from 1836 to 1843. During that time he was referred to as the holiest man in Scotland. Wave upon wave of spiritual power flowed from his sermons. Crowds came hours ahead of time to hear the Scriptures expounded by the silver-tongued youth. Revival fires sprang up wherever he preached. Even during the last months of his life when his chest was racked with a tearing consumptive cough, he delivered the message of Christ. Even in his delirium he talked about Christ.

He died when he was barely thirty. On the day of his funeral, business houses closed in respect. Torrents of tears poured from the eyes of weeping thousands who had been blessed by his ministry.

Later when Robert McCheyne's memoirs were published, the Christian world learned that David's prayers and untimely death had brought Robert to Christ.

But for David's faithful intercession, Scotland might have been denied her greatest minister, the saintly Robert Murray McCheyne.

The Frightened Skeptic

Adoniram Judson

"Jacob, I agree with you. The Bible is no different from the Koran or the other sacred scriptures of the world. Jesus Christ was only a good man. But I cannot tell my parents. At least, not for a while."

Adoniram Judson, honor student at Brown University, was talking to his closest friend, Jacob Eames. Adoniram's father, pastor of the Third Congregational Church of Plymouth, had sent him to Brown with great hopes. Adoniram had consistently led his class in grades, but he had also fallen into company with Jacob Eames, a persuasive unbeliever.

At graduation time, Adoniram's parents proudly rode down to Providence to see their nineteen-year-old son receive the valedictory honors. Adoniram dazzled the audience with his valedictory address on the subject of free enquiry, but he never so much as hinted to his parents that he had become an unbeliever.

Back home in the parsonage, young Adoniram opened the Plymouth Independent Academy. Each day after teaching the children of local blue bloods, he turned his energies to writing. By the following summer he had two textbooks ready for publication.

All the while he played the hypocrite, piously taking part in family worship and faithfully attending church on Sunday. As he reflected upon his hypocrisy, he felt sickened and bored.

"I should like to go to New York and write for the stage," he announced to his parents one day.

He had anticipated their reaction. New York in 1807, to godly Congregationalists, was the final touch of depravity. They reacted as if he had announced his decision to commit suicide.

They reasoned, begged, and mildly threatened him. Finally, the elder Mr. Judson said with a bit of exasperation, "Why don't you study to be a minister, if you don't like teaching?"

At that Adoniram was infuriated. He poured out the truth that their God was not his God, that he did not believe in the Bible or the divinity of Christ.

They were shocked and deeply disturbed. His father argued with him. His mother begged and prayed with tears.

In the end, Adoniram won out. Tall and straight, he rode toward Albany to take passage to New York.

The steamship on which he booked passage, the *Clérmont,* was the first successful steamboat in American history. But this was no omen for its passenger. There was no fortune or fame for him in New York. After a few weeks of a vagabond's life, he traveled back to an uncle's home, secured a horse, and rode west, sure only that he would not return to Plymouth and his father's parsonage. When night drew on, he took lodging at a village inn.

"I have a room, but it's next to one in which a young man is critically ill," the landlord said. "He might die during the night."

Adoniram was unimpressed. He needed a place to rest.

But rest did not come for him. Through the night he heard the sounds in the next room—low voices, people moving about on the creaking floor, weird moans and gasps. He could not stop thinking about death. How would he face the enemy which his father would welcome as the doorway to God? His philosophy had no answer, beyond earthly life.

Sleep finally came in the early morning hours. He awoke with sunlight streaming through his window. But there was no sunlight in his heart. He trudged wearily downstairs and asked for his bill.

"How is the sick man?" he asked, trying to sound casual.

"Dead." The innkeeper hardly looked up when he replied.

"Too bad," Adoniram replied respectfully. "Did you know him?"

The innkeeper's words sent Adoniram's mind reeling. "A fellow from the college in Providence. He registered as Jacob Eames."

Adoniram rode away along a country road. Where was his old friend, Jacob Eames, now that he had died? Suddenly he had the feeling that his father's God was true—that Jacob Eames' beliefs had failed him. He reined in his horse, whirled the animal around, and galloped toward Plymouth.

Back home, Adoniram weighed the arguments for the truth of his father's faith. It took several long sessions with some distinguished Christian thinkers, but finally he was assured in his mind and heart that the

Bible was true. On a bleak day in December—one he never forgot—he dedicated himself fully to God.

His dedication led him into the ministry. The largest church in Boston sought his services. But his dedication went further than Boston.

Twelve days after his marriage to beautiful Ann Hasseltine, he sailed with his bride to Burma.

There he toiled for six years before rejoicing in his first convert. He labored on despite the death of his loved ones, and despite imprisonment and torture by the Burmese king.

In 1850, the year of his death, he completed the first Burmese Bible and finished most of the first Burmese-English dictionary. In the years afterward, abundant fruit came from his labors. By the one-hundredth anniversary of his death, missionaries had counted almost two hundred thousand Christians in Burma—a glorious tribute to the young scholar who had found faith after the death of his skeptical college friend.

The Transformed Thief

George Müller

The grim-faced Prussian tax collector confronted his ten-year-old son. "You have taken money which is not your own, George."

The boy squirmed under his father's gaze. "No, Papa," he stammered. "I took no money."

"This time I set a trap," the father explained. "I thought you had been sneaking from my tax collections, so I counted a sum and left it in this room. Some of it is gone. Now the cat couldn't have taken it."

"You made a mistake, Papa," the boy pleaded.

"I made no mistake. If you will not admit it, then I must search you."

The tax collector went through his son's pockets and found nothing. George smiled smugly.

"Now remove your shoes," his father commanded.

"My foot hurts. It will pain my foot."

"Remove them, I said."

The boy reluctantly removed his shoes.

"Now hand them to me."

The boy obeyed. The smile had frozen uncertainly on his face.

"Ah, here it is. Now, to the woodshed with you."

"But Papa, I'm sorry. I promise not to steal again."

George Müller took his punishment. But he did

steal again, and again, and again—until his life was changed by Christ.

His mother died when he was fourteen and away at school. The night that she was dying, being unaware of her illness, George was playing cards. He spent the next day, a Sunday, at a tavern with some friends.

A short while later he was confirmed in a Lutheran church. His father had given him a handsome fee to pay the clergyman. But wily George gave the clergyman only one twelfth of the amount.

"I will do better," he promised himself as he participated in the service. But his resolution proved to be in vain.

The following year, his father was transferred to the town of Schoenebeck, Prussia. He left George at the old home alone to supervise some repairs and to study with a clergyman, since George had decided to study for the ministry. But while the tax collector was gone, George was busy with other business. He collected money which the villagers owed his father for taxes, then took a trip which he later called "six days of sin."

When his money was exhausted, he moved into an expensive hotel, stayed a week, then sneaked out without paying the bill. He moved to another hotel, stayed for a week of fun, then prepared to escape through a window. But this time he was caught. At the age of sixteen, the tax collector's son was in jail where he stayed for twenty-four days.

After his father bailed him out, he entered school at Nordhausen, Prussia. To the delight of his teacher he studied from four in the morning until ten at night. The teacher held him up to the class as a young man with great promise in the ministry. But George Müller's drinking and debauchery continued. He had twinges of guilt when he partook of the Lord's supper. "But one or two days after partaking I was as bad as ever," he wrote in his journal.

When he was twenty, he was recommended to the University of Halle and granted the privilege of preaching. It was at Halle that he realized he must reform if a parish was to ever choose him as pastor. At that time he looked upon the ministry merely as a good living, not as a service to needy humanity.

He met a fellow student named Beta who seemed to live an exemplary Christian life. George chose Beta as a close friend, thinking that he could improve his life with a Christian companion.

But Beta was a backslider and had entered into George's friendship only because he thought George would introduce him to more pleasures.

In August, 1825, George Müller, Beta, and two other students, pawned some of their belongings to get enough money for a few days of travel. When one of the students suggested Switzerland, the wily George had a plan ready. He simply sat down and forged the necessary letters from their parents with which to get passports.

On the trip George carried the purse. And, thief that he was, he manipulated the funds so that his companions paid part of his own expenses.

Back at the university, Beta was stricken with remorse and made a full confession of his sins to his father. He then invited George to attend a cottage meeting at the home of a friend.

They went together. "I had never before seen anyone on his knees in prayer," commented George, who later was to become world famous for his own power in prayer.

George felt awkward at the meeting with its strange atmosphere. He even apologized for being there.

"Come as often as you please; house and heart are open to you," the host invited him pleasantly.

After two hymns, a chapter in the Bible was read. Then another hymn, and while the host prayed, an inward joy and peace was springing up in George Müller's heart. On the way home, he excitedly told Beta, "All our former pleasures are as nothing compared to what we experienced tonight."

Christ had touched George Müller's heart at the cottage meeting, and from henceforth he lived a transformed life.

Later he moved to England, where he became widely known as the man of faith. He founded five orphan homes in Bristol with shelter for two thousand children. During his lifetime he cared for 9,975 orphans and received one and a half million dollars by faith alone. Before his death he estimated he had received fifty thousand specific answers to prayer.

This was the man who never saw a Christian kneel in prayer until he was twenty-one.

The Troubled Gardener

Robert Moffat

"Aye, Robert, I don't know what's a-comin' to ye."
And with that lament, the Scottish schoolmaster "Wully" Mitchell laid on the rod. Robert Moffat grimaced
and took his punishment, vowing to know his Presbyterian catechism next time.

But there were ships to watch and sailors' tales to
hear, and each time he was called upon to recite from
his catechism, he seemed to merit only the teacher's
rod.

Robert lived only a few miles from Edinburgh, and
when he was ten, a friendly captain took him on several voyages. Robert's ship had some hairbreadth escapes along the rocky coast, too many for even the
boy's adventuresome spirit. He hurried back home,
sadder and wiser.

He endured a few more months of school, picked up
a little knowledge of geography and astronomy from
his older brother, then at the age of fourteen was apprenticed to a gardener.

The work was hard. He rose from the shed where
he slept and started his day's planting, spading, and
stoking hothouse fires, at four A.M. Often it was so
cold he had to rap his knuckles against his spade handle to bring feeling into them.

Four years later, Robert received a job offer from the High Legh estate in Cheshire, England. His parents bade him a tearful farewell. He promised to read a chapter from the Bible every morning and evening.

At the estate he was given a shed and the responsibilities of tending nineteen fires in the greenhouses. He stoked in the morning and banked in the evening. In between he pored over the books in his mistress' library. A thirst for knowledge was at last filling his mind.

He also had another thirst brought on by his daily Bible readings. He found a small group of Methodists meeting on a corner of the estate property. The class had been organized in 1783 by one of John Wesley's zealous preachers. The young gardener enjoyed the informal studies, until he became disturbed about his own spiritual condition.

As he tended his plants, the question, "What think ye of Christ?" kept disturbing him. One night he had a frightful dream. His sins seemed to pile up into a great mountain which was rolling down upon him. He awoke, shivering, and fell on his knees, but when he tried to pray, a black cloud seemed to fall over him.

Robert wanted desperately to have the conversion experience which the Methodists talked about, yet it seemed he could not.

"Perhaps," he thought, "if I were a great sinner I could have a great experience with Christ." But he was unable to force himself to do that which his godly mother had so earnestly warned him against.

Then he tried the opposite tack of forsaking foolish and worldly company, vain thoughts, and wicked imaginations. Still his mountain of sins loomed up before him.

Confiding in no one, he wrestled with his burden in the isolation of his hedges and flowers. Later he wrote, "I tried to hear Jesus saying to my soul, 'Only believe;' but the passages from which I sought comfort only seemed to deepen my wounds."

But Robert Moffat's day of peace did come . One night while meditating on the epistle to the Romans, the familiar passages seemed to give light he had never seen before. Of this experience, he testified, "The Book of God . . . seemed to be laid open and I saw what God had done for the sinner. . . . I felt that, being justified by faith, I had peace with God through the Lord Jesus Christ."

Soon after his conversion, his employers offered him the position of head gardener with several men under his direction. There was one stipulation, that he give up the Methodist meetings which they disliked.

But Robert Moffat's convictions had been whetted on the divine grindstone. "I thank you for your good intentions," he replied candidly, "but I would prefer my God to white and yellow ore."

A few days later he saw a poster by the town bridge advertising a missionary meeting. Over and over he read the announcement. And, there the resolve came "to go to sea again and get landed on some island or foreign shore where I might teach poor heathen to know the Saviour." The poster had brought back memories of missionary stories which his mother had read to him back in Scotland.

From that moment on, Robert Moffat's heart was set

on a missionary career. He applied to a missionary society but was rejected because he was not promising enough.

Reverend William Roby, a missionary-minded minister, disagreed with the society. Taking young Robert under his tutelage, he helped him secure employment with a Christian man who needed a gardener. Robert could support himself and at the same time further his education for the mission field.

All went well until Robert and his employer's daughter fell in love. Mary Smith's parents agreed to a marriage, but only if Robert gave up his intentions of becoming a missionary. The two lovers labored and prayed over their problem for hours. Finally, they agreed that Robert must fulfill God's call at whatever cost it took. Mary would wait and hope that her parents might relent.

In the year 1816, Robert Moffat departed alone for Africa. Before leaving, he wrote to his parents, "Oh, that I had a thousand lives and a thousand bodies!"

Two years later, Mary Smith's parents finally consented to the marriage, and Mary sailed across the Atlantic. In Capetown, South Africa, she and Robert had a joyful reunion and were married.

Robert and Mary Moffat spent fifty-two years of pioneer mission service together before returning to England at the age of seventy-five. They put down the foundations and set the pattern for mission work throughout the dark continent. Thousands were converted through their ministry. Fierce tribal chieftains became peace-loving. Robert Moffat became the first to translate and print Christian literature for Africans in their own tongue.

From the sparks that flashed from Robert Moffat's heart, another Englishman caught fire for Africa. This was the great David Livingstone, who married Moffat's daughter, Mary, and following his father-in-law, opened up vast jungles of the great continent for spiritual conquests.

The Father of Faith Missions

Hudson Taylor

Before Hudson Taylor was five he was saying, "When I become a man, I will be a missionary and go to China."

The English boy's sensitive heart had been impressed by stories about the lands where almost no one had heard about the true God. But those who knew young Hudson passed it off as only childish impulse. William Carey had gone to India, and a few others had taken the gospel to foreign lands, but the notion still persisted in English church circles that God would convert the heathen Himself when he was ready.

The Taylor home was both happy and godly. Each day James Taylor read a Bible passage and explained it to his children. "God cannot lie," he would often tell them. "He cannot mislead you," and little Hudson would bob his curly head as if to say, "Surely it is true if Father says so."

But the simple trust of childhood slipped away as Hudson entered his teens. For six years he was unsettled spiritually. He tried hard to "make himself a Christian" by performing every religious exercise that came to his mind. *Surely,* he thought, *there is some way I can become worthy of God's love.*

He began working in his father's apothecary, mixing

and dispensing medicines to the customers, but he was still not sure that he had taken the right spiritual medicine for his soul. At work one day, he read a tract story of a half-wit who was able only to fix his mind upon one spiritual truth—that Christ came to save sinners—and in that truth he found peace that sustained him in death.

After reading the tract, Hudson quietly bowed his head and made his first conscious attempt to surrender to Christ. But in later years he did not consider this to be a true conversion.

When he was fifteen, he secured employment as a junior bank clerk. Most of his associates in the bank seldom spoke of religion without a sneering wisecrack. An older clerk who befriended him took every opportunity to laugh at Hudson's old-fashioned notions.

Despite his better judgment, Hudson permitted his mind to be dragged into cynical disdain of his childhood teaching. "I began to set too great a value on the things of this world. Religious duties became irksome to me," he later wrote.

But Providence was working. Working long hours by gaslight resulted in serious inflammation of his eyes. Nothing seemed to help his failing eyesight, so after nine months in the bank, he again became his father's assistant.

He confided to his parents that he was not sure of the truth of what they had taught him. They tried to be patient with him. His mother and younger sister Amelia redoubled their prayers.

One day he was at home alone. During the afternoon he explored his father's library, looking for a book to help him pass the time. But no book seemed interesting; so he turned to a basket of religious pamphlets. Selecting one, he told himself, "There will be a story at the beginning and a sermon at the end. I will take the story and leave the sermon."

What Hudson Taylor did not know then was that seventy miles away, his absent mother was kneeling in prayer for him. After the noon meal she had felt an intense concern for Hudson's conversion. Locking herself in a room, she had resolved not to leave the spot until being assured her prayers were answered.

Meanwhile, Hudson had come upon the phrase, "the finished work of Christ." "Why should not the author say the atoning work of Christ?" he asked himself. Immediately the words of Jesus on the cross, "It is finished," shot into his mind.

Then came the further thought, "If Christ has finished paying the debt for my sins, what is there left for me to do?"

And with this came the happy assurance that there was nothing he could do, except fall on his knees and accept what Christ had done.

Two weeks later his mother arrived home. Embracing her, he told her the good news. "I know," she said happily, "I have been rejoicing for a fortnight. God assured me that my prayers were answered."

Thus began a long life of spiritual victory for Hudson Taylor. He did go to China as a missionary. He founded the great China Inland Mission which has been responsible for putting thousands of missionaries on spiritually needy fields. Many have called Hudson Taylor the father of faith missions.

The Case of the Skeptical Lawyer

Charles Finney

"If Christianity is true, why don't you convert Finney?" a young farmer asked his zealous Christian wife. "If he's converted, I'll believe." The farmer was only one of many young people in the upstate town of Adams, New York, who were hiding behind the coattails of the popular young bachelor lawyer.

Charles Finney was admired for both his physical and intellectual prowess. As a sixteen-year-old schoolmaster he had won the admiration of his frontier scholars by out-running, out-wrestling and out-jumping them all. He became a musician, then a classical scholar, then a lawyer at twenty-six. By the year 1821, when Finney was twenty-nine, he had a booming practice and was the idol of the town's young people.

Everyone was aware of Finney's skeptical views. He argued with the minister, but because of his musical talent he served as choir leader at the Adams Presbyterian Church. Once in a prayer meeting he was asked if he wanted to be prayed for. "I suppose so," he countered half-heartedly. "But you have already prayed enough in this church to pray the devil out of Adams—if there's any virtue in your praying."

But the choir leader's caustic remarks did not keep a small band of the church young people from praying for him. And, unknown to them, conviction began its work.

Finney's favorite reading menu was Blackstone's law books. He noticed the prized volumes repeatedly referred to the Bible as the highest authority. He bought a Bible, partly for his own education and partly to help him outwit his pastor. After several weeks he became convinced that the Bible was not to blame for the inconsistencies he saw among the religious people he knew.

Finally he decided to make his peace with God.

On a Monday he methodically began reading his Bible—this time for spiritual help. But each time he heard a client knock on his door, he covered his Bible with law books. When he decided to pray, he plugged the keyhole of his office door to keep from being heard outside. These sly attempts to find peace, however, brought him no relief.

Wednesday morning arrived, and he padded into his law office, eyes hollow from loss of sleep. Suddenly an inner voice seemed to whisper, *What are you waiting for? Are you trying to become righteous on your own?* Writing later he said, "I saw then that Christ's work was a finished work . . . and that all I must do was consent to give up my sins and accept Him."

Finney closed his office for the day. He slipped away into the woods and found an outdoor closet formed by several large, fallen trees. As he knelt, he heard the leaves rustle. He looked up, embarrassed that someone might find him on his knees. But no one was there. He remained in the solitude to pray.

It was noon when he walked out of the woods. His heart was singing. He went back to his office, knelt in earnest prayer, and received a mighty infilling of the Spirit. Afterward almost the entire town was converted—including all but one of the young people. He preached in a nearby village named Sodom where the only good man in town was called Lot. And like the town of Adams, Sodom bowed to Christ before Finney's testimony.

Dozens of other New England communities bent under the gale force of his empowered preaching. His ministry spread to the big cities. Ten thousand were converted in a series of meetings in Rochester. He went on to become a famous evangelist, professor, college president, and pastor. Today his lectures and memoirs are standard reading in evangelical schools. The once skeptical lawyer became a highly influential factor in American Christianity.

The Boy Who Was Afraid of God

A. B. Simpson

Young Albert Simpson cast an envious glance at the strip of sunlight seeping through the transom. Then he cautiously tiptoed toward the door and with one hand on the door latch, he cast a wary glance over his shoulder. His father was not watching. Quickly he pulled the latch and scampered outside.

A few moments in the warm Ontario sunshine was enough to make him forget that this was the Sabbath. But a shout from the doorway brought him back to reality.

"Boy!"

His father's beckoning hand sent a chill racing along his spine. He had been caught, and now he would be punished.

"Today is the holy Sabbath," the old Scot thundered. "But you'll not get the rod today."

Young Albert heaved a sigh of relief.

"Tomorrow morn, ye can be prepared."

The cloud of gloom moved over Albert again. He shuffled inside, knowing that at the crack of dawn, the whip would crack on his back.

Albert's back was still smarting the next day, when

his older brother passed along a secret tip. The next time Albert had a whipping coming in the morning, he followed his brother's advice.

He arose a few moments before his father, lit a candle, and sat down in a corner of the living room. He opened the Bible and pretended to be reading. Then, as his father entered the room, Albert stared at the Bible with the most penitent and pious look he could summon. Just as the older brother had predicted, Albert's father did not even mention the whipping.

But, a short while after this incident, Albert Simpson was in no mood for fooling his father. At fourteen he had had a nervous breakdown from the strain of studying too hard. His doctor had told him not to look at a book for another year.

Following his collapse, Albert called for his father. "Pray for me," he begged. "I'm dying, and I'm afraid to face God."

Later Albert Simpson wrote of this experience, "I had no personal hope in Christ. My whole religious training had left me without any conception of the simple gospel of Jesus Christ. The God I knew was a being of great severity."

After his father prayed, Albert tried to pray also but with little faith. That night he feared to go to sleep lest he should lose a moment in his search for God.

Slowly his health returned, but the peace of God continued to elude him. His father read the Bible to him and prayed but never explained that salvation was free for the asking. The old Scot Calvinist held firmly to the belief that God must act in some dramatic way if Albert were to be saved.

Finally Albert stumbled upon a musty old book in

his minister's library, *Marshall's Gospel Mystery of Sanctification*. His eyes fell upon a life-awakening sentence: "The first good work you will ever perform is to believe on the Lord Jesus Christ. Until you do this, all your works, prayers, tears, and good resolutions are in vain."

The light dawned! Albert Simpson fell to his knees crying, "Lord, I dare to believe that Thou wilt receive me and save me because I have taken Thee at Thy Word."

A few days later he wrote out a long and detailed covenant which he called, "The Dedication of Myself to God." In it he said, "Thou hast subdued my rebellious heart by Thy love. Take it now and use it for Thy glory." At that time, January 19, 1861, Albert Simpson was barely seventeen years of age.

Before his conversion, Albert had felt he must enter the ministry to please God. Now he wanted to preach the gospel because of the joy that filled his heart.

He entered Knox College in Toronto and graduated as a brilliant and gifted minister at the age of twenty-one. Immediately, the Knox Presbyterian Church in Hamilton, Ontario extended a pastoral call. The church had a seating capacity for twelve hundred worshipers, and soon the boy preacher was attracting capacity audiences.

After eight successful years in Hamilton, Albert was called to become the minister of the Chestnut Street Presbyterian Church in Louisville, Kentucky, which at the time was one of the largest churches in North America.

His preaching again attracted capacity audiences. On Sunday evenings he moved the church services to the public library hall which seated more than two thousand.

More spiritual success followed Albert Simpson when he moved to become pastor of the great Thirteenth Street Presbyterian Church of New York City. But after two years there, he told the congregation, "You want a conventional church for respectable Christians. I want a multitude of publicans and sinners." Whereupon he resigned, rented a hall in a needy section of town, and began preaching to his "publicans and sinners."

Only seven were present at the first service, but from this group grew the great Christian and Missionary Alliance. Albert B. Simpson is honored today as the founder of this great missionary fellowship.

In 1963, the C.M.A. celebrated its seventy-fifth anniversary. The records showed slightly less than one hundred thousand members in the United States supporting 876 full-time foreign missionaries. No other evangelical denomination has as many missionaries in ratio to members, on the foreign field.

Life in a Look

Charles Haddon Spurgeon

Knowing that both his father and grandfather were famous English ministers was not much help to troubled fifteen-year-old Charles.

"I thought my sins were greater than other people's," he wailed. "I cried to God for mercy, but I feared He would not pardon me."

While he was attending school in Colchester, young Charles vowed, "I'll attend every church in town to find out how to become a Christian."

He heard one sermon on Galatians 6:7, "Be not deceived, God is not mocked." But the preacher did not say how he might avoid deception. After six months of visiting every chapel he could find, he was almost in despair.

Then came the cold, snowy morning of January 6, 1850. Dutifully, Charles set out to attend the church he had selected. As he trudged along, his heart felt colder than the falling snow. When he saw that the fierce storm would prevent him from reaching his destination, he turned aside to an obscure chapel he never before knew existed.

At first he was hesitant to enter the Artillery Street Primitive Methodist Church. Later he said, "I had heard that those people sang so loud they made one's head ache."

But Charles Spurgeon slipped in and sat down. After several minutes of painful silence, a tall, thin man shuffled to the pulpit. "Looks as if our minister was held up by the weather," he explained. "Reckon you'll have to put up with me."

"Now I'll take a text like all preachers do," the homely man continued. "Look unto me, and be ye saved, all the ends of the earth" (Is 45:22). Sitting in his pew, Charles grimaced and thought, *Why, he can't even pronounce his words properly.*

Up front, the substitute preacher began spinning his text around, for he knew of little else to say. "The text says 'Look,'" he droned. "Now, lookin' don't take a deal of pains. It ain't liftin' your foot or finger; it is just 'Look'!

"Now some of ye are lookin' to yourselves, but it's no use lookin' there. Ye may say, 'Wait for the Spirit's workin.' But I say, look to Christ."

The eyes of the bored handful of hearers began to wander, but not Charles Spurgeon's. He was staring at the ignorant preacher as if to say, "Why didn't I think of this before?"

As the preacher rolled his text along, he began shouting, "Look unto Me, I'm sweatin' great drops of blood; I'm hangin' on the cross." Then the tall man spotted Charles' strained face.

"Young man, you look miserable," he thundered, as the boy slid down an inch in the uncomfortable pew. Then he lifted up his hands and shouted in Primitive Methodist style, "Young man, look to Jesus Christ. Look! Look!"

Charles later testified, "I saw at once the way of salvation. I looked until I could have almost looked my eyes away. The darkness rolled away, and I saw the sun. I felt I could spring from my seat and shout with the wildest of these Methodist brethren, 'I am forgiven.' "

"Oh, how I wish I could do something for Christ," Charles wrote to his mother after he returned home. Within a week, he was doing something. First it was giving out tracts; then when his supply was exhausted, he wrote on slips of paper, and dropped them on the streets, hoping someone could be helped.

He began teaching Sunday school at sixteen and a year later was called as pastor at Waterbeach Chapel. Then he moved to London and a larger church, and before he was twenty-one, he was acclaimed "the boy wonder of England." At twenty-three he preached to exactly 23,645 people in one service. His church built the Metropolitan Tabernacle that seated fifty-five hundred people. He founded a college for preachers, an orphanage, and even a gospel paper. His sermons were published by American newspapers. And still today— one hundred years later—many believe Charles Haddon Spurgeon to be the greatest preacher since the apostle Paul.

In 1864, Spurgeon revisited the Artillery Street Chapel. He preached from the text, Isaiah 45:22, through which he was converted. Pointing to a seat under the gallery, he said, "I was sitting in that pew."

The true identity of the tall, thin substitute preacher is still shrouded in mystery. He never came forward to acknowledge that he delivered the sermon that prompted the great Spurgeon to look to Christ.

In a Moment of Despair

Reuben A. Torrey

He was a freshman at Yale at fifteen. His banker
father had important social connections back home in
Brooklyn. His quick mind learned easily without much
study. He was an expert dancer with an engaging way
with the girls. His conscience was not overly sensitive
about campus good times.

"What more could a fellow want?" Reuben Torrey
asked himself. And during his few months at the university, he always smiled back at himself in the mirror
and said. "I've got all I need to make me happy."

But the one discordant note was his praying mother.
Just to think of her prayers made Reuben feel uncomfortable. She wanted him to become a Christian. To
Reuben, his mother's definition of the Christian life
was giving up everything that he enjoyed—dancing, social drinking, card playing, and other worldly delights.

He thought he had settled the matter a few years
back. He was in the attic of the family mansion and
came across an old book that explained how to become
a Christian. For the first few pages he agreed with
everything the book said. God loved him. Yes, he could
accept that. God gave His Son to die for mankind's
sins. Yes, that was true. A person could receive forgiveness by believing in Christ. This seemed to be no
problem.

But then he read, "To become a Christian you must surrender your life completely to God's will—go wherever He wants you to go, do whatever He wants you to do."

Reuben had slammed the book down then. God would want him to give up the race track, card playing, and dancing. He might want him to be a preacher instead of a lawyer. There certainly would not be any joy in all that, he decided.

As a student at Yale, he was bothered again. As the days passed, his life became tasteless. He felt hollow inside when he laughed. Too often his smiles were forced.

Then one night he dreamed that his mother was dead. She came to him as an angel saying, "Reuben, won't you become a minister of the gospel?"

In his dream, Reuben promised his mother that he would be a preacher. Then he awoke with a start, painfully conscious of his dream promise.

His melancholy increased. Frequently he lapsed into moments of despair. One night he had a sudden impulse to commit suicide. He hurried to the washstand and fumbled for his razor or any other sharp instrument that would serve his purpose. But he could not find a suitable weapon.

Then suddenly he snapped back to reality and an understanding of what he had almost done. "O God," he moaned, dropping to his knees. "Deliver me from this burden. I'll even preach."

Sometime later he got back into bed. He drifted off to peaceful sleep with a soothing peace settling over his mind.

From that time on, Reuben Torrey was settled on

becoming a minister of the gospel. In the Yale chapel, he made a public profession of faith, and following his graduation, he entered the Yale divinity school.

While in seminary, Reuben Torrey heard the man whom the students had called a strange, uneducated evangelist. After D. L. Moody spoke, Torrey and some other students asked him, "Tell us how to win people to Jesus Christ."

The plain-spoken Moody replied in his usual blunt manner, "Go at it. That's the best way to learn."

Then Torrey heard Moody say in another sermon, "Faith can do anything." And Reuben Torrey said to himself, "He is right. No man has ever accomplished anything for God who did not have mighty faith."

Reuben A. Torrey made faith the keynote of his life. After a successful ministry in Minneapolis, he was invited by D. L. Moody to become superintendent of the Chicago Bible Institute, known today as Moody Bible Institute. Torrey soon became known as Moody's right-hand man, and after the evangelist's death, he took over the leadership in American evangelism.

In 1902, Torrey and Charles Alexander began their famous round-the-world revival campaign. In Australia, New Zealand, and India, twenty thousand converts were reaped. In Great Britain, where they spent three years, seventy-five thousand answered Torrey's call to repentance.

Torrey was not only a power in evangelism, but he was known worldwide for his skill and brilliance in Bible teaching and writing. His practical books on the Holy Spirit, prayer, and evangelism are still being read by thousands of Christians.

The Cricket Champion Finds Christ

C. T. Studd

"Wonder what the old man's got planned for us," C. T. Studd mused to his brothers as their carriage rolled out of the academy grounds.

"We'll have a sporting good time, that's for sure," C. T.'s older brother, George, remarked. "There's not a fellow back at old Eton that wouldn't like to be in our shoes."

"Agreed, brother, agreed," C. T. and Kynaston said.

The boys passed time on the trip home by remembering old times. They talked about the steeplechases their wealthy sportsman father had won and especially about the time when his horse, Salamander, had won the Grand National.

Edward Studd, the boys' father, met them with a bright gleam in his eyes. C. T. and his two brothers leaped from the coach and extended hearty handshakes.

"Well, where are we going, Dad?" C. T. asked jovially. "The minstrel show, the circus, the theater?"

Mr. Studd grinned as he shook his head. "Something new," he chortled.

A short while later, Mr. Studd stopped his carriage in front of a hall. C. T. looked at the poster on the building and groaned, "Moody and Sankey, the American revivalists."

Edward Studd smiled broadly at his sons. "Boys, I might as well tell you now. I've been converted by Mr. Moody. No more racing and gambling. I've found the real thing."

C. T. and his two brothers followed their father inside, too amazed to answer. They listened to the bearded evangelist but made no move when the call was made for the inquiry room.

Back at the country mansion, C. T.'s father told the boys how he had become a Christian and had given up racing. Then he declared that he was giving each of them a race horse. The other horses in the stable would be sold. C. T. and his brothers looked at one another in amazement. This was incredible. As long as they could remember, racing had been their father's greatest delight.

C. T. was immediately aware that his father wanted his sons to be converted too. After a few conversations, C. T. began pretending sleep each time the bedroom door opened. During the day he tried never to let his father find him alone.

A year passed. The boys came home again for the summer holidays. They looked forward to some exciting cricket matches at the family estate. As they had expected, their father had preachers staying at the house each weekend.

One weekend, two preachers came. The boys discovered that one, Mr. W., was not a good rider. Keeping a straight face, C. T. insisted that Mr. W. go for a ride.

Mr. W. and one of the boys rode in front; the two others behind. Suddenly, without warning, the two behind galloped past like the wind. Mr. W.'s horse leaped after them. The unfortunate guest hung on for dear life while the brothers almost split their sides laughing.

But the guest had his revenge. During the afternoon he caught C. T. on his way to play cricket.

"Are you a Christian?" he asked.

"Yes, I believe in Jesus Christ and the church, too," C. T. replied, hoping to shake his pursuer off.

"Look here at this verse," the guest said showing him John 3:16. "Do you believe Jesus Christ died for you?"

C. T. nodded impatiently.

"Do you believe the last half of the verse—that the one believing has everlasting life?"

C. T. Studd blinked before saying, "I don't think I can believe that."

"Well, then either you or God is wrong," the persistent man declared. "Do you think God is not telling the truth?"

"No."

"Then you're inconsistent in believing only half of the verse," Mr. W. continued. "Are you always going to be that way?"

C. T. bit his lower lip. "I should be consistent. Yes, I will be."

The guest pressed his point. "Eternal life is a gift, don't you see? Will you get down on your knees and thank God for his gift?"

C. T. nervously looked around. He knew the man was right. Down on his knees he went. And when he arose, his heart was filled with joy and peace. Religion with him had ceased to be a weekend dread.

That same weekend, Mr. W. won all three brothers

to Christ. All three became outstanding witnesses for the gospel which Moody and Sankey had brought to England.

Shortly after his conversion, C. T. Studd enrolled in Cambridge where he starred in cricket and became known as England's greatest cricketeer. He was the best known athlete of his day.

At the height of his athletic popularity and prowess, he announced his decision to go to China as a missionary. He also gave away to Christian causes his entire personal fortune of about one hundred thousand English pounds. After serving in China for ten years, he toured American college campuses, raising hundreds of mission volunteers in the Student Volunteer Movement. In 1910, he went to Africa and began work in the region between the Nile and Lake Chad, the largest unevangelized region in Africa at that time. C. T. Studd died in 1931. Today he is remembered as one of the greatest Christian missionaries of modern times.

The Shepherd's Dog

John Vassar

"No, Matthew, I won't go," John Vassar told his cousin, adding a curse for emphasis.

His cousin turned to walk away, then on a second thought, turned around. A glittering gold piece was in his hand.

"It's worth this to me for you to hear the gospel."

John Vassar had recently married. He could use the money. "Sure. Why not?"

That night John fell under deep conviction. On his job at the brewery the next day, he sulked, moodily struggling to curb his profanity and temper.

A few evenings later, he arrived home to find his wife already asleep. Shaking her bed, he cried, "How can you rest when your husband is going to hell?"

No one had to pay him to return to church. He went at every opportunity. Then, one night in March 1842, he was sitting in a rear pew of the Lafayette Street Church in Poughkeepsie, New York. The service closed, and the people began filing out. "Stay and pray with me," John Vassar pleaded.

A group huddled around him and prayed. Reverend Rufus Babock, the pastor, laid a hand on his quivering shoulder. "John, look to Christ. It's faith that saves you, man, not feeling."

"I will," John Vassar murmured. "He is my only hope."

By the next evening, it was plain that he had trusted Christ. His face shone. "I've found peace at last," he told a prayer meeting group.

Afterward, he walked home singing hymns with some friends. On the way one remarked, "We'd better be quiet. People will think us crazy."

"Let them," John Vassar spoke up happily. "They said Jesus had a devil."

The statement was a portent of his future. For the next thirty-seven years "Uncle" John Vassar, as he was best known, spoke up for Jesus—sometimes with such zeal and frankness that less earnest Christians called him crazy.

He was thrust forth into his work when his wife and two children were taken by disease. Never ordained, he called himself the Shepherd's Dog, trekking from church to church praying for and winning the lost sheep. The American Tract Society gave him a small salary for colporteur work.

During the Civil War, he witnessed to the Union soldiers in the front lines. In one brigade where he worked as an unofficial chaplain, an estimated one tenth of the men were converted.

His power in prayer was widely publicized. Once he was captured by the Confederates. Put on trial before General Stuart for being a spy, he turned the tables by asking, "General, sir, do you love Jesus?"

General Stuart was relieved when an aid took him aside to whisper, "Get rid of that man, or we'll have a prayer meeting from here to Richmond."

When Uncle John grappled with a soul, he began

by striking home with the most direct question possible. When there was no chance for a long conversation, he left a single piercing verse of Scripture.

Once a student returning home met him on the road and inquired his business. "I'm looking for some lost sheep," Uncle John replied. When he arrived at home, the youth told his parents about the crazy man searching for sheep.

"Why that's Uncle John Vassar, the tract missionary," they responded smiling. "He's searching for people to win to Christ."

When Uncle John died in 1878, he was accounted the most skillful personal soul-winner in America. No one doubted that the price his cousin paid to get him to church was worthwhile.

When a Mission Cheated Lake Michigan

Mel Trotter

On a rugged, cold night in January, a man staggered through the streets of Chicago intent on ending his life in the icy waters of Lake Michigan. But on Van Buren Street God intervened, and the man was pulled through the doors of the Pacific Garden Mission.

Harry Monroe, an excounterfeiter, was leading the singing when he saw the youthful drunkard being ushered to a seat. Abruptly he stopped the music. "Let us pray," he said. "O God, save that poor, poor boy."

Mel Trotter's head jerked erect when he heard the prayer. After that he managed to hear part of the testimonies and preaching. Through it all, his head reeled with the aching memories of his past.

His father was a saloon keeper and a drunkard. Mel often tended the bar. At nineteen he started drinking and betting on "sure shots" until he finally lost his job.

Then when he married, he promised his bride that he would never drink again.

But one night after a long drive Mel went to stable his horse. Suddenly a devilish desire swept over him. Without saying goodbye to his wife, he pushed the horse back out into the snowstorm. When he returned he had averaged a drink a mile with three quarts left for home consumption.

His next reformation held up for eleven and one-half sober weeks. When he weakened, he sold his horse for drinks.

He moved to the city where his sober spells became shorter and less frequent. "I'll quit," he vowed more times than he could remember. But he didn't. He began staying away from home for weeks at a time, even stealing to quench his thirst.

Mel was hospitalized and given treatment for alcoholism. When he was discharged, he was given a medicine kit. After fifteen minutes on the street, he traded the kit for three drinks of whiskey.

He did not even stop drinking when his wife gave birth to a baby boy. One day after a ten-day drinking spree, Mel came home to find his dead son in his wife's arms. Overcome with grief and guilt because of his neglect, he decided to kill himself.

His wife put the lifeless infant down and dropped to her knees in prayer. Then she arose and pulled Mel into her arms, turning him from suicide.

"I'll never take another drop," he promised as hot tears streamed down his face. But two hours after the baby's funeral, Mel Trotter staggered home—drunk again.

On the night of January 19, 1897, with all this behind him, Mel Trotter started toward Lake Michigan to drown himself. He never arrived there, however, because he was pulled into a mission.

There he heard Harry Monroe, the superintendent,

tell of how God had saved him from a life of drunkenness and counterfeiting.

At the close of the service, Monroe gave an invitation. "Jesus loves you," he said, looking squarely at Mel. "Make room in your heart for Him tonight."

Mel Trotter jumped to his feet and moved forward. Harry Monroe pointed him to Christ.

Afterward, Mel spent every night he could in the mission. Sometimes he played the guitar and sang gospel songs. Frequently he and Harry Monroe visited churches in the Chicago area as a team.

Three years after his conversion, Mel Trotter was appointed superintendent of a rescue mission in Grand Rapids, Michigan, where he spent forty years in fruitful ministry. During that time he used the fifteen-hundred seat Grand Rapids mission as a base to start sixty-six other gospel lighthouses in this country—all designed to reach the down and outer for Christ.

All this happened when a rescue mission cheated Lake Michigan out of a suicide victim.

The Prisoner's Joy

Jeremiah McAuley

"Jeremiah McAuley, you are sentenced to serve fifteen years of hard labor in Sing Sing Prison."

The words of the austere judge were still ringing in his ears when Jerry McAuley saw the story of his life—"The way of the transgressor is hard"—engraved over the prison entrance.

His father had been a counterfeiter. At thirteen Jerry took his first lessons in crime. At nineteen he was a river thief and the terror of the New York waterfront. Ironically, he was innocent of the robbery charge that sent him to Sing Sing. His underworld associates had framed him with trumped-up evidence.

For four years he hated the men who sent him to prison and dreamed of his escape. Then, one morning, as he and the other prisoners filed into chapel, he recognized an old friend on the platform. The surprise almost tumbled him to the floor.

"That's Awful Gardner! What's he doin' up there?" he muttered.

When his old friend came down on the floor to speak to the men, Jerry listened in amazement. "I was wearing stripes like you only a few months ago," Awful explained. "Then I found Christ as my Saviour and—" A rain of tears blocked his flow of words. Awful

Gardner knelt in prayer, but sobbed and cried so loud that the prisoners could hardly understand his words.

Jerry McAuley looked uneasily around him, then furtively raised his hand to wipe his tears away. Then, as if under a spell, Jerry listened to the speaker tell how he had become a Christian.

Back in his cell Jerry beat the dust from his Bible. Then for the next few weeks he used every free moment for Bible reading.

Inside he was fighting a battle with his sin. Even though he wanted to pray, it just did not seem that he could. Then an inner voice whispered, "Remember the prayer of the publican."

Jerry McAuley fell on his knees, but instantly sprang up to see if someone was watching. He dropped down again, cried to God for help, then jumped up, still ashamed. His conflict continued until one night he fell on the cold stone floor, not caring if anyone watched. "I'll stay here all night if necessary to find forgiveness," he vowed. But that was unnecessary.

In his agony he saw Christ hanging on the cross and he seemed to hear Him say, "My son, thy sins are forgiven."

His body quivered with the thrill of new life. He jumped up, clapped his hands, and shouted, "Praise God! Praise God!"

A guard was passing in the corridor. "What's going on in there?" he yelled.

"I've found Christ," Jerry shouted.

"Be quiet, or I'll report you in the morning," the guard threatened.

But Jerry McAuley's witness was not to be silenced so easily. First he won his friend Jack Dare, then several other prisoners, before the governor granted him a pardon and he walked out a free man.

When Jerry returned to New York, he found society reluctant to accept an exconvict, even though he had been converted. He fell back into some of his old habits for a while. Then a city missionary found him penniless and wandering the streets. He gave Jerry spiritual counsel and helped him find employment.

Jerry McAuley had a vision. He had a house in the waterfront district. He resolved to use that place to start a rescue mission for men like himself who were cast down and needed a helping hand. As people came, he ministered to their physical needs and led them to God to remedy their spiritual needs.

In October 1872, at 316 Water Street, Jerry opened the Helping Hand Mission. Inspired by his success in winning down and outers to Christ, other zealous Christians began starting missions all across America. One of Jerry's converts, Colonel H. H. Hadley, started sixty-two rescue missions himself.

Jerry McAuley, the man who found joy in prison, died on September 18, 1884. But the rescue mission movement he helped to spark continues on.

The Curious Rabbi's Son

Solomon Ginsburg

Thirteen-year-old Solomon Ginsburg sat proudly listening to the discussions of the rabbis who had come to help his father celebrate the Feast of Tabernacles.

The talk lulled, and Solomon's eye fell upon a well-worn copy of the Prophets. He casually opened the ancient writings to the book of Isaiah, chapter 53. In the margin was scribbled a question: "To whom does the prophet refer in this chapter?"

Solomon innocently read the question to his father, who was also a rabbi.

His father remained silent. Solomon repeated the question, thinking he had not heard. Without speaking, his father slapped his face and angrily closed the book.

Two years later, young Solomon Ginsburg was in London where he found employment with an uncle. He had run away from his home in Poland because his father had insisted he become engaged to a twelve-year-old girl.

One afternoon while walking on Whitechapel Street he met a Jewish missionary.

"Are you Jewish?" the missionary inquired.

"Yes," Solomon replied proudly.

"Then you will be interested in my sermon tonight at the Mildmay Mission. It will be from Isaiah, chapter 53. Would you come?"

Solomon's heart leaped as he remembered the episode with his father. "Yes, I will," he promised.

That evening the Jewish boy slipped into a rear seat at the mission. The missionary reverently read the prophecy, then painstakingly showed proof from the New Testament that Jesus was the suffering Messiah of which the passage spoke. Afterward he walked to where Solomon was sitting. "Do you believe?" he asked pointedly.

"I don't know," Solomon replied. "You see, my father is a rabbi."

"Read the New Testament," the missionary suggested. "Then ask yourself if Jesus is the Messiah predicted in Isaiah 53."

Solomon promised that he would. By the time he reached the crucifixion account, he was weeping. As he read Matthew 27:25, "His blood be on us, and on our children," he was trembling as he thought of his people who had rejected the Messiah. Then he recalled the curse that was placed upon Jews who deserted the orthodox faith. He knew that his entire family would disown him.

For three months Solomon Ginsburg struggled. Then he heard a sermon on Matthew 10:37, "He that loveth father or mother more than me is not worthy of me."

When the preacher asked for testimonies he stood to say, "I want to be worthy of Jesus."

His load was lifted. But the die of his future was already cast.

"Why do you look so happy, boy?" his uncle asked the next morning at breakfast.

"Uncle," he announced forthrightly, "I have accepted Jesus as my Messiah."

His uncle paled and left the table. When Solomon made a public profession of faith, his relatives responded by discharging him from employment and putting him on the street with only the clothes he was wearing. Then news came from his family that he was disinherited and disowned by them. Another relative came and read to him the solemn excommunication ceremony of curses.

His family had completely turned their backs on him, but Solomon Ginsburg did not turn his back upon his newfound Messiah. He enrolled in the Regions Beyond Mission College, graduated, and went to Brazil as a missionary in 1890. For the next thirty-one years, he served valiantly in pioneer mission work. Although he was persecuted, stoned, and even imprisoned for his missionary efforts, he saw his denomination grow from less than a thousand to more than twenty-one thousand in number during his ministry.

Country Bumpkin in the City

Dwight L. Moody

Dwight was a rough and tumble boy who left his farm home at seventeen to work in his uncle's shoe store in Boston. One of his uncle Samuel's requirements was "Sunday school and church every Sunday."

His Sunday school class was well sprinkled with Harvard boys. Dwight, who could neither spell nor read well, called the other members of the class, "those rich and pious parishioners."

Reluctantly, the young shoe salesman enrolled. Then one day his teacher, Edward Kimball, brought a lesson on Moses. The country bumpkin listened entranced. When Mr. Kimball finished, Dwight spoke up in his customary brusque manner. "That Moses was what you'd call a pretty smart man."

The Harvard boys covered their faces but could not choke back their snickers.

A few Sundays later, Mr. Kimball handed Dwight a Bible as he announced the lesson from John. Dwight took the book in his big, thick hands and began fumbling in Genesis. The teacher saw out of the corner of his eyes that the others were smirking and punching one another. Quickly he frowned at them and passed Dwight his Bible opened at the proper place.

Dwight did not forget the embarrassment. He vowed,

"If I ever get out of this scrape, I'll never be caught there again."

The next Sunday he was absent. The teacher went after him and begged him to return. Dwight was persuaded and promised to begin reading two chapters a day to avoid future embarrassment.

During the worship service, he usually sat in the gallery. One morning when he dropped off to sleep, a young Harvard man gave him a solid jab with his elbow. Dwight awoke, rubbed his eyes, and looked down at the minister. Perspiration beaded out all over him and he said later, "I never felt so cheap in my life."

After a year of bumbling and embarrassment, Dwight was getting better in his reading. On April 21, 1855, Edward Kimball felt the time had arrived to talk to his country pupil about Christ.

The teacher, quite timid himself, arrived at the shoe store, hesitated at the door, then walked away with a second thought that it might be better to wait.

He was half a block down the street when he overcame his reluctance. He dashed back up the street and burst into the store. Dwight was in the rear, wrapping up shoes.

Edward Kimball leaned over and put his foot on a shoe box. With his hand on Dwight's shoulder he began as best he could. "I want to tell you how much Christ loved you."

A few moments later, the boy, who was the best salesman in the store, had melted. The time was ripe. Unknown to his teacher, he had been trying to become a better person. He had even gone so far as to sign his resolution in his own blood.

When Kimball asked if he would surrender to Christ, Dwight mumbled a tearful but happy yes.

Later Dwight told about how he felt. "I was in a new world. The birds sang sweeter. The sun shone brighter. I'd never known such peace."

As soon as possible he made a visit to his Northfield, Massachusetts, farm home. There he eagerly gave his Christian testimony, feeling sure that his six brothers and two sisters would immediately want what he had. But they did not respond, and he returned to Boston discouraged.

More discouragement came when he applied to join the Mount Vernon Church. The membership committee decided he should wait. They were not sure he had really been converted.

But even this did not quench young Dwight's zeal. When he spoke up eagerly at the midweek prayer meeting, a deacon took him aside to advise, "You can serve the Lord better by keeping still." He was finally admitted to church membership about a year later.

Dwight Moody moved west to Chicago and made a small fortune selling shoes on Lake Street. He spent his weekends ferreting out slum district youths for a Sunday school he had started on Chicago's north side. He became such a success in his missionary endeavors that he left the business world to become a full-time Christian worker.

Over fifty years after his death, the *Chicago Tribune* honored the former country boy from Massachusetts with the editorial comment: "Dwight L. Moody deserves to be remembered as the greatest evangelist of the nineteenth century."

Quest of the Gypsies

Gipsy Smith

Cornelius Smith was an English gypsy. Usually he kept only three steps ahead of the law. Sometimes he was caught for pitching the family tent on a lord's estate or letting his horses graze on a farmer's crops. Then would come the inevitable jail term. He never had enough money to pay his fine.

Smith first heard the gospel from the lips of a prison chaplain. Back in his cell, he cried, but there was no one to guide him.

When his term ended, he soon was busy making trinkets, fiddling in the liquor shops, and endlessly moving on in hopes of greater opportunities. He forgot all about the chaplain's message until the day his wife died of smallpox.

"I'm trying to pray," she gasped. "But I keep seeing a black hand coming before me showing me my sins."

Cornelius tried to tell his wife what he had heard in prison. She listened, then smiled.

"I believe," she said. "Be a good father to my children." He promised that he would. Then she died.

Cornelius and his motherless brood of six set out across the meadows. Often his children overheard him saying, "I don't know how to be good. How will I get my burden taken away?"

Soon Cornelius was visited by his two brothers, Woodlock and Bartholomew. "Brothers," Cornelius confided, "I have a burden of sin I must get moved."

To his astonishment the brothers answered, "We feel the same way. We have a burden. But who will help us? We poor gypsies cannot read."

"Let's go to London town and find a church," Cornelius suggested.

"Agreed."

On the way the three brothers stopped at a tavern. "Can you tell us how to have our sins forgiven?" they asked the lady innkeeper.

"Oh, my soul," she groaned. "I have been troubled about my sins. But I have a book upstairs that might help you."

The book was *Pilgrim's Progress*. When they reached the place where Pilgrim's burden dropped off as he gazed at the cross, one brother cried, "That's what I long for. I want my burden taken away."

A few nights later they neared London. Cornelius put his horses into a farmer's field, intending to take them out before daybreak. That night he dreamed of Christ. Holding up nail-pierced hands the figure said, "I suffered this for you. When you surrender all, I will save you."

When he took his horses from the field the next morning, he vowed never to sin willingly again.

"Where can I find a gospel meeting?" he asked a road worker.

"I'll take you to one tonight on Latimer Road," the worker offered.

Cornelius, his children, and his brothers went to church. The people were singing, "I do believe, I will believe, that Jesus died for me," when Cornelius fell to the floor. A few moments later he rose up shouting, "I'm converted! I'm converted!" At this, his son Rodney ran out of the church, thinking his father had gone crazy.

Brother Bartholomew also was converted that evening. He and Cornelius went back to their tents singing heartily, "I do believe, I will believe, that Jesus died for me."

Then brother Woodlock found Christ. The three brothers formed a gypsy evangelistic team and went roaming over the countryside to preach and sing the gospel.

Cornelius' son sixteen-year-old Rodney, noticed the change in his father's life. He came to trust the Saviour a few years later and declared, "God has called me to preach."

In the year 1876, Rodney taught himself to read with a Bible and an English dictionary. He practiced preaching in a turnip patch.

Today Rodney is remembered as Gipsy Smith, the world famous evangelist who shook two continents for Christ.

Billy Sunday Finds Home Base

Billy Sunday

The Chicago White Stocking's big right fielder wobbled out of a Chicago tavern. With him were five of his buddies. "Where to now?" one stammered, as Bill Sunday lurched to a stop on Van Buren Street.

Pointing to a band of street musicians, Bill said, "Let's listen to the music." The fact that his name was a household word among Chicago sports lovers did not keep him from plopping down right then on the curbstone of the busy street.

For some time, Sunday and his teammates listened to the music. Sunday was the most interested, for the musicians were playing hymns he had heard his mother sing in their log cabin back in Iowa.

Then the music stopped. "We are from the Pacific Garden Mission," Harry Monroe, the group's spokesman said. "The service there begins in a few minutes. Come with us, and enjoy the singing and preaching."

"Hey, Bill, what's going on here?" His teammates began to jeer and snicker. One jostled him in the ribs. But something was happening. Bill Sunday's bleary eyes were beginning to clear.

"Come hear how drunkards become sober and harlots pure," Harry Monroe was saying. "Come. Come." And with that the band launched into another hymn, keeping cadence with their feet as they marched off toward the famous mission.

Bill Sunday jumped to his feet. "I'm going to Jesus Christ, boys," he said with jaw set. "Come with me if you'd like."

As Sunday strode away, four of his teammates guffawed loudly. One of them did not laugh. Instead, he slapped Bill on the shoulder. "More power to you, boy."

Bill Sunday went to the mission that night. He listened, but he made no definite decision other than to return. To his surprise, most of his teammates were sympathetic when he turned up for practice the next day. He went back to the mission again and again. Finally one night in conversation with Mrs. Clarke, wife of the mission's founder, Bill Sunday said yes to Christ.

That was the year 1886. Sunday continued with the White Stockings team, only instead of playing ball on Sundays, he spoke to boys at the YMCA in the city where his team was playing. The hero-worshiping youngsters thronged to hear the man who was fast becoming a legendary base stealer in baseball. At that time he was known as the "fastest man in the leagues," being able to circle the bases in fourteen seconds.

Five years after Sunday's conversion, the Chicago club released him at his insistence. The Cincinnati team immediately offered him $500 a month. But Sunday took a job at the Chicago "Y" as an assistant secretary in the religious department. His salary was only $83.33 per month, on which he had to support his wife, daugher, and invalid brother. To make ends meet, he walked to work and back each day, had his old clothes dyed to appear new, and wore a celluloid collar.

But a few years later, Bill Sunday, better known as "Billy," became a world-famous evangelist. In one ten week series of meetings in New York, 98,264 persons "hit the sawdust trail" to grip the big athlete's hand and say yes to Christ.

When the baseball evangelist died in 1935, the number of converts from his ministry had swelled to an estimated one million, with another one hundred million who had heard him preach.

Message from the Dying

Sam Jones

The curtains were drawn. Inside the sick chamber a mother lay dying. A thin, sallow-faced boy stepped to her side.

"I need you, Mother," he begged, while struggling to hold back the tears. "Don't leave yet."

Her voice was gentle. "Sam, I will never be able to return to you." She gasped for breath, then almost like a prayer added, "But you can come to me."

Sam Jones never forgot the words of his dying mother.

Just before he was scheduled to enter college, he became ill. Even though his father was a Methodist minister, he began drinking, thinking that alcohol would help his "nervous stomach."

Then he rallied, and in between spells of drinking he began studying law. He was admitted to the Georgia bar in 1868, and called, by a judge, "the brightest boy ever admitted to our state's bar."

He married a lovely girl, but his drinking increased. When he was sober enough to try a case, he was aclaimed, "Sam Jones, the brilliant lawyer." Too many other times he was "Sam Jones, the drunkard."

News came to Sam while he was on a six-week drinking binge that his father was seriously ill. He hurried to his bedside.

"How are you, Dad?" the prodigal said, trying to hide his breath.

"I'm weak in the body, boy," the man of God replied. "But spiritually I'm strong. When every other prop fails me, Jesus stands firm."

Sam squirmed uneasily. He had been one of the props that had failed.

His father grew weaker. The relatives were called in to say good-bye. Sam stood at the foot of the bed listening to the farewell messages. When his father asked for him, he moved to the head of the bed.

"My poor, wayward boy," the dying man gasped. "You have broken the heart of your wife and have brought me in sorrow to my grave."

Sam looked away as salty tears flooded his bloodshot eyes.

"Promise me you'll meet me in heaven."

Overcome with emotion, Sam took his dying father's hand. "I promise!" he shouted. "I'll quit drinking and set things straight. I'll meet you and Mother in heaven."

His father died. Sam never took another drink. The following Sunday he went to hear his grandfather preach. At the close of the sermon, he went forward requesting the prayers of the church.

He continued to listen to his grandfather's sermons. A few weeks later he plodded up the aisle again, saying, "I want to give all that is left of me to Christ."

One week later, Sam Jones delivered his first sermon from his grandfather's pulpit. That began a long career in evangelism.

114

Sam Jones was popular with saint and sinner alike. He was best known for his colorful language. Like, "Many a fellow is praying for rain with his tub bottom side up"; and, "It tickles me to see an old sinner come in and pull out an old, dwarfed member of the church, lay him down and measure by him, and say, 'Look here, boys. I'm as long, as broad, and as good as this man.'"

From Boston to San Francisco, great crowds flocked to hear him preach. Thousands were converted through his ministry. D. L. Moody once took time off just to hear Sam Jones preach. President Theodore Roosevelt asked for his counsel.

Sam Jones, the drunken lawyer, became Sam Jones, the evangelist, who, as one admirer said, "put the fodder down low where the poor folks can reach it."

Why Preacher Pulliam Returned

George W. Truett

"He can beat anybody at gettin' music from folks at a singing bee," the mountain people declared. "And you ought to hear how he tamed the twenty-year-old bullies at Crooked Creek School where he's schoolmaster," they usually added.

Youthful George Truett, handy with plow, rifle, and books, was easily the most popular boy in Clay County, North Carolina. But though he was a regular churchgoer, all his admirers knew well enough that he was not a Christian.

Now it was Sunday morning preaching time at Clay County Baptist Church. George was squirming on his bench, eagerly waiting for the visiting evangelist to finish his sermon and close the revival. George knew that the persuasive Preacher Pulliam had almost roped him into the Lord's corral.

Finally the evangelist finished his sermon and, to George's relief, said his good-byes. The pastor announced the customary evening services, and George and his family filed out with the other worshipers.

That evening, George Truett was back at the church his family had attended for as long as he could remember. But when it came time for the sermon, the revival preacher unexpectedly returned.

116

After a short whispered conversation, the pastor said, "Brother Pulliam feels compelled of the Lord to continue the meetings here for another week." A solemn hush fell over the congregation.

Preacher Pulliam took Hebrews 10:38 for his text, "The just shall live by faith: but if any man draw back, my soul shall have no pleasure in him."

George Truett, the young mountain teacher, sat as though pegged to the hard church seat. As the preacher spoke, he was remembering the times God had spoken to him.

When he was only six, he had felt a deep need for God's forgiveness while listening to a country preacher. That night in his little bed he yearned for someone to tell him how his sins could be forgiven.

There had been the time he was looking for his father's cows and was almost bitten by a deadly rattlesnake. On the way home, a mountaineer told him, "You were lucky to git out of that cove alive. Three years ago I helped kill seventy-two rattlers up there." George had breathed a prayer of thankfulness and hurried on home.

At age eleven the Spirit had called him again during a revival meeting in the mountain church house. But there was "time enough yet," he had assured himself.

Now George Truett had entered young manhood. He sat tensely, listening to Preacher Pulliam warn of the peril of trifling with Christ's call. When the sermon was over and the invitation hymn begun, George was one of the stream of people who went forward to surrender publicly to the Saviour.

The next morning at the breakfast table, George and his mother talked about the great decision he had made. "Last night, after coming home from the meeting, I put myself to a test," he told the one who had prayed for him since before he was born. "I said to myself, *What if Christ should now come visibly to me and ask: 'Are you willing from this time on to let Me have My way with your life? Are you willing to trust My way as always being best?'*"

"How did you answer, son?"

"I answered yes without any reservations," he said. "Afterward, my heart was filled with a great peace."

Wednesday night of the extended week of revival came, and the pastor spoke to George. "There are many people here who are near to becoming Christians, but they are hesitating. Will you say a word of exhortation?"

George's knees were shaking when he got up and gave an appeal. But a moment after he started, he was out in the aisle pleading personally with friends and neighbors. Then suddenly he thought, *What a fool I am making of myself!* Feeling humiliated, he sat down, but not before many of the hill folks had sought God's mercy.

Later when George W. Truett had become one of America's greatest preachers, he said, "From that hour, people began telling me, 'Shouldn't you give your life to the gospel ministry?'"

Not long after George's conversion, the Truett family moved to Whiteright, Texas. George's talents were soon recognized, and he was elected superintendent of the Baptist Sunday school. George often conducted services himself, always standing in front of the pulpit because he felt unworthy to stand behind it.

Many times he was urged to enter the ministry. Each

time he solemnly answered, "I will speak for Christ, but I am not worthy to be His minister." Finally the congregation called a special meeting.

At the Saturday night meeting, the oldest deacon rose to say, "We feel that this church has a duty to perform. We have waited far too long already." Then while the young superintendent listened with amazement, the deacon stated his motion, "I move that this church ordain Brother George W. Truett to the full work of the gospel ministry."

George Truett rose to his feet in protest. But the members' pleadings forced him to relent. The following morning he was ordained.

The wisdom of the church's decision was proven in the years ahead. A few weeks after his ordination, the persuasive young Truett, at only twenty-three was appointed to lead the fund-raising drive that lifted Baylor University from crushing debt. When he graduated from Baylor he was offered its presidency, but he declined in favor of the pastoral ministry.

For over forty years he served as pastor of the First Baptist Church of Dallas, becoming the best-known Texan of his time. During his ministry the church grew to become the largest church in Texas and in the Southern Baptist Convention. Three times he was elected president of his denomination, and in 1934, he was elected to the highest office in the worldwide Baptist fellowship, President of the Baptist World Alliance.

This was the mountain boy who became a Christian because Preacher Pulliam was responsive to the Spirit and extended his revival.

Harry Lad Is Born Again

Harry Ironside

Harry Ironside was a remarkable boy!

At three he memorized his first scripture verse—one he did not learn the real meaning of for many years—"For the Son of man is come to seek and to save that which was lost" (Lk 19:10).

During his eighth year he read the Bible all the way through, reading three chapters on weekdays and five on Sundays. The next year he read the Bible through twice, and by the time he was fourteen he had caught up with himself by having read it through a total of fourteen times.

When his widowed mother moved from Toronto to Los Angeles, eleven-year-old Harry discovered there was no Sunday school in the neighborhood where they lived. But this was a challenge instead of a problem for him.

He gathered together the children in the neighborhood. After outlining his plans, he sent the boys out to collect all the cloth sacks and burlap bags they could find. Then he organized the girls into a sewing club. In a matter of days the youngsters had erected a burlap tent that would easily cover a hundred people. During the first year the average attendance was sixty. Harry was the teacher.

Sometimes a few adults would come to the burlap tent Sunday school. After listening to Harry, they would come up, pat him on the head, and say, "God bless you, little preacher." Nothing pleased Harry more.

When Harry was twelve, Mr. Moody came to town. Harry was late for the first night of the 1888 Los Angeles Crusade. He found every seat taken in Hazzard's Pavilion so he walked up to the second gallery and found room in a trough-like girder that joined the gallery to the roof.

High up in his perch, Harry listened to the bearded evangelist preach. And while he listened he prayed, "Lord, help me some day to preach to crowds like these." He did not even dream then that forty-two years later he would be pastor of the church which Moody founded.

After Moody left, Harry continued his Sunday school work. One day when he was fourteen he came home from school to find a visitor waiting.

"Harry, you remember Mr. Munro, the evangelist," his mother said. "He visited us in Toronto."

Indeed, Harry did remember. Donald Munro, a tall man with a long brown beard, had stayed in the Ironside home on numerous occasions. And every time he had asked Harry at least once, "Lad, are you born again?" Harry's stock reply was that he memorized Scripture, gave out tracts, and went to Sunday school.

And Mr. Munro's retort always was, "Oh, laddie, you can do all that and still spend eternity in hell."

Now after a four-year absence, his old tormenter had caught up with him again. And, as Harry expected, his question was the same as before.

121

"My, my, how you've grown, Harry, lad," the bearded preacher chortled. "Now tell me, are you born again yet, laddie?"

Harry blushed and stared down at the floor. Then his uncle Allan, who was present, interrupted, and Harry thought he was rescued.

"Didn't you know, sir? Harry preaches himself now. Has his own Sunday school."

But the bearded visitor only expressed amazement, "You mean you're preaching and not yet born again! Get your Bible, lad. We've some things to talk about."

Harry reluctantly dragged himself upstairs. A few moments later he shuffled back down.

"Now, lad, read Romans 3:19," Mr. Munro instructed.

Harry read the verse. "Now we know that what things soever the law saith, it saith to them who are under the law: that every mouth may be stopped, and all the world may become guilty before God."

"Now, lad," the visitor commented. "When God makes a preacher, He stops his mouth first and shows him his lost condition. Then God leads him to put His trust in the Lord Jesus and He is born again. Don't you think you've been putting the cart before the horse?"

"Maybe so," Harry answered weakly in a not-too-positive tone.

A few weeks later, Harry became more positive that he was going at things backward. He gave up his Sunday school, telling himself that if he was not a true Christian, he had no right to speak for God. Then the thought came, *Since you're not a Christian, why not enjoy all the things you've stayed away from before?*

122

So Harry went out to have a good time in the world. But every time he did, he came home with a burning conscience. About six months later, Harry was attending a merry party of young people. Suddenly a verse of Scripture he had learned came to his mind: "Turn you at my reproof: behold, I will pour out my spirit unto you, I will make known my words unto you. Because I have called and ye refused; . . . I will mock when your fear cometh . . . as desolation, and your destruction cometh as a whirlwind . . . Then shall they call upon me, but I will not answer; they shall seek me early, but they shall not find me" (Pr 1:23, 24; 26-28).

As never before, fourteen-year-old Harry felt the pangs of his guilt before God. He saw what he had been doing. As soon as he could manage an exit, he hurried home to the privacy of his room.

He arrived after midnight and turned immediately to his Bible. First he turned to Romans 3, a chapter Mr. Munro had asked him to read. Then he turned back to John 3 and read about the new birth. He knew this chapter by memory, but this time the words stuck to his heart. His fingers moved over John 3:16 and "whosoever believeth in him should not perish, but have everlasting life," and verse 18, "He that believeth on him is not condemned."

Then he declared aloud, "I believe, Lord. This verse says I'm not condemned if I believe."

But he felt no different. He read the verses over again. This time he said as resolutely as he knew how, "Lord, I rest on Thy promise. I do now take Christ as my Saviour, and because Thy Word says so, I know I have eternal life."

At long last, Harry Ironside had been born again.

The years ahead were fruitful ones for Harry Ironside. He became known around the world for his skill in Bible exposition. For many years he was pastor of the great Moody Memorial Church in Chicago. He wrote over twenty popular commentaries on books of the Bible, and authored dozens of other booklets and gospel tracts. But in all of his sermons and writings he never grew tired of telling of how Harry, lad had been born again.

God Saves a Future President

James A. Garfield

"God, keep Your hand on little Jim," the Widow Garfield prayed. The three older children by the fireplace murmured their amens. Little Jim, going on three, grinned his approval. He was too young to fully understand, yet the nightly prayers gave him a warm feeling of security.

His father had died the year before, leaving his mother to feed the family and take care of the frontier farm near Orange, Ohio. But with God's help and the help of the children, she managed. Before Jim was twelve he was doing a man's work—chopping wood, planting crops, hoeing corn, and cradling wheat.

When he reached sixteen, Jim went to Cleveland to seek a job. Fresh in his hearing was the prayer of his mother, "Keep Your hand on Jim."

Jim's cousin, captain on an Erie Canal boat, gave him a deckhand's job. On Jim's first trip to Pittsburg, he fell into the canal fourteen times. On the second trip he accidentally flipped a setting pole into a burly deckhand. The big man, twice Jim's age, rushed toward him with a curse. Jim neatly stepped aside and floored the attacker with a strong blow behind the ear. The bully was tamed, but Jim's troubles were far from over.

A few weeks later, the boat, named the *Evening Star*, was coming out of a stretch of slack water. The bowline had caught in a crevice on the deck's edge. Jim was trying to jerk it out of the crevice, when suddenly the rope came loose. The boy's momentum threw him over the side and into the water.

His heavy oilcloth coat and pants pulled him toward the bottom. He felt the boat gliding over him. The whole crew was asleep and Jim could not swim. Then his thrashing hands touched the dangling rope. He grasped it tightly and moments later had pulled himself back on the deck. Standing there dripping wet, Jim saw that the rope had again caught in a crevice, thus providing him the lifeline. Amazed and awed, he threw the rope six hundred times at the crevice without success. Finally he said, "Only God could have put that rope there. He must have saved me for something better than canaling."

But when Jim returned home, malaria struck him down. He battled with the disease for six months while his widowed mother prayed, "God keep Your hand on Jim."

When Jim recovered from malaria, he enrolled at Geauga Academy with plans of becoming a teacher. He worked as a carpenter's helper to pay school expenses and provide needed money for his mother at home.

After two terms, Jim took a temporary teaching job near his log home. Beside his skill at taming bullies, the young teacher was known for his regular church attendance. When the local Disciples church held a revival meeting, Jim Garfield was on hand. On March

126

4, 1850, he answered the preacher's invitation to accept Christ as his Saviour. Six days later he wrote, "The cause of God is prospering. In this place seventeen have made the good confession and are rejoicing in the hope of eternal life. Thanks be to God for His goodness. By the help of God I'll praise my Maker while I have breath."

A few months later, the man who would one day be president, wrote: "When I consider the sequel of my history thus far, I can see the providence of God in a striking manner. Two years ago I had become ripe for ruin. On the canal . . . ready to drink in every species of vice . . . I was taken sick; unable to labor, went to school two terms . . . took a school in the winter; and greatest of all, obeyed the gospel. Thus by the providence of God I am what I am. . . . I thank Him."

After his conversion, James A. Garfield moved ahead fast. He went to Williams College in Massachusetts and studied under the famous Mark Hopkins. After graduation he was given a professor's post at Hiram College, then a year later at twenty-six, he became president of the school. On weekends he served as a lay preacher in nearby churches.

At twenty-eight, he became the youngest member of the Ohio Senate. He served in the Civil War so illustriously that President Lincoln made him a major general. Next came Congress and in 1879, a seat in the US Senate. But before he could begin his term, he was nominated to the nation's highest office.

Shortly before his nomination, Garfield left the political convention to attend church. He told a friend, "Yes, this is a day of suspense, but it is also a day of prayer; and I have more faith in the prayers that will go up from Christian hearts today than in all the tactics which will prevail at this convention."

Garfield defeated Winfield Hancock in a close election. Then leaders of his own party turned against him because he refused to give office jobs to politicians whom he considered unqualified. Garfield favored a system of governmental promotions based on merit, later adopted and known today as civil service.

After only six months in office he was shot by a mentally deranged job seeker. Near death, he whispered, "God's will be done, doctor. I am ready to go if my time has come."

The Captain's Sword

Russell Conwell

"Son, will you lead us in prayer this morning and give thanks for your safe trip home?"

Slowly young Russell Conwell shook his head.

"Have your studies at Yale caused you to forget?" The old man's question was edged with disappointment.

The youth hung his head and stared into his plate. He coughed uneasily.

"Speak out, boy, What is wrong with you?"

"I no longer believe your way, Father. I cannot pray to a God in whom I do not believe."

Russell Conwell's parents gripped their chairs in disbelief. Life on the Massachusetts farm had been hard. But their boy had been cradled in the Bible and family prayers. He had been a devout church attendant.

"I've joined the Infidel Club at Yale," the youth continued, breaking the tense silence. Then seeing the tears of his parents, he added, "It's not that I don't love and respect you. You're the most wonderful parents a boy could have. But when I got to college, I saw all those rich boys with money to burn. And I had to eat the leftovers given to me for helping the dormitory cook. Well, it didn't seem right."

"What didn't seem right, son?"

"That God should let us be so poor. Some of those rich students couldn't care less about religion. And yet, Dad, you and Mother have always tried to serve God— the God in whom I just can't believe anymore."

Tears welled up in the eyes of the farmer and his wife. There was a long, uncomfortable silence during which no one spoke. Russell Conwell noticed that the work-worn hands of his father were trembling although they rested on the table. "Son," the father finally began, "I would rather see you in your coffin, or live in ignorance, than for you to forsake God."

Russell Conwell went back to Yale and continued working to pay his way. By the time he received his degree, the country had been plunged into the Civil War.

Young Conwell immediately became an ardent spokesman for the cause of Union victory. He gave public lectures on the life and death of John Brown. He recruited a company of volunteers, was appointed their captain, though only nineteen, and marched off to war.

Captain Conwell soon became a hero for his bravery and daring. In tribute, his admirers presented to him a glittering gold-sheathed sword, which bore the Latin inscription, *Vera amicitia est sempiterna*—"True friendship is eternal." He did not know then that the sword would play a prominent part in changing his life.

Shortly before the presentation of the sword, a Boston customs house employee sought out Captain Conwell. "My boy Johnny is determined to go to war," he told him. "I should like to trust him into your hands."

The captain eyed the scrawny, awkward-looking

teenage boy. "Boy, are you willing to lie on the ground all night and have your hair frozen to the ground? Are you willing to have an arm or leg shot off for your country?"

The boy nodded.

"Then if you still want to go, I'm willing to make you my personal servant."

Johnny Ring shared his captain's tent, sleeping across from his cot. On his first night with the captain, he took his Testament from his pocket and prepared to read by the light of their army lantern.

Captain Conwell saw what Johnny Ring was doing. "Put that away!" he shouted in sudden rage. "We don't believe the Bible around here. I gave up such foolishness long ago."

"But, sir," the boy protested. "I promised my mother when she was dying that I would read my Testament every night."

The captain calmed a bit. "I respect your love for your mother. But if the other officers see you reading here they will rag me to death about it. Go outside the tent."

Johnny Ring put his Testament away. He could not see to read it outside by the flickering campfire. After that, he waited until the captain was out of the tent. But one evening the captain walked in early.

"Johnny, I asked you not to read the Bible in here," he fumed. "Now, as your superior officer, I command you to stop."

The boy burst into tears. As he lifted the door flap, he turned to face his unbelieving captain. "Captain, sir, I love you. But you are a wicked man."

A few weeks later their regiment was ordered to an

occupied area near New Berne, North Carolina. Their job was to guard a railroad line that ran from New Berne to the coast.

One dark night, Captain Conwell was checking the sentries he had posted at the edge of the woods. A bullet zinged out of the darkness and knocked him to the ground. Miraculously, the bullet smashed only the watch in his pocket.

Shortly afterward, he rode into New Berne on business. While he was there, he received word that General Pickett's Confederates had captured his encampment, setting fire to the camp and the nearby railroad bridge.

"What happened to my servant, Johnny Ring?" he asked the courier.

The messenger's smoke-blackened face lit up in admiration. "Well, sir, as we retreated across the burning bridge, Johnny Ring shouted, 'The captain's sword is in his tent.'

"We yelled for him to come back, but, sir, that boy streaked across the bridge and snatched your sword from the blazing tent. As he came back across the bridge the battle was fully under way."

"The Confederates killed him, then?"

"No, sir. The Confederate commander nearest the bridge ordered his men to cease firing. We all watched Johnny as he ran with your sword. Finally he reached our side and fell to the ground. His uniform was blazing, but he had your sword. We rolled him in the river to put out the fire. He has been taken to the Army hospital at Beaufort, North Carolina."

The captain learned later that when Johnny Ring regained consciousness in the hospital he asked, "Has the captain got his sword?" A nurse assured him it was there beside the bed. Johnny asked to touch it, and said, "I'm glad I saved it." Then he asked, "Is Captain Conwell coming to see me?" They told him that word had been sent.

During the night the surgeon called the chaplain to the bedside. Johnny Ring was dying. "You are going to see your mother, son," the chaplain whispered. "Don't be afraid to go."

The dying boy whispered back, "I'm not afraid. But I wish I could see the captain once more."

The hospital told Captain Conwell what Johnny Ring had said. The sword was returned with its motto, "True friendship is eternal."

Captain Conwell looked at the polished weapon and read the words. *Will I ever see Johnny again?"* he asked himself. *And my parents? They believed in eternal things. If I could only see Johnny to beg his forgiveness for my ill-treatment.*

The war moved on. Captain Conwell rose to the rank of lieutenant colonel. But still the memory of loyal Johnny Ring haunted him.

The battle of Kenesaw Mountain near Atlanta came. Lieutenant Colonel Russell Conwell was in the forefront when he was hit by an exploding shell. He was wounded so severely that his men left him for dead.

The following morning, the cleanup detail found him alive. In the hospital at Marietta, Georgia, the staff debated about amputating his arm. Only a nurse's objection saved it.

A Baptist chaplain paused by his bed. They talked long enough for the chaplain to discover the colonel's doubts.

"Colonel, you know by instinct that there is life after death," he said. Then gently, step by step, the chaplain led the wounded officer to surrender his life to Christ.

Afterward he gripped the chaplain's hand and whispered, "I must serve God, not only for myself, but for Johnny Ring." From that day until his death, Russell Conwell led the life of a devout Christian.

After the war, Russell Conwell's star of influence rose rapidly in the world. He moved to Minneapolis and established the *Minneapolis Chronicle,* which is today the *Tribune.* He was admitted to the bar as a lawyer. And he lectured and worked in Sunday schools.

Then a dark cloud of failing health settled upon his horizon. He consented to surgery in New York. The surgeon removed from his lungs a grisly souvenir of his war days. Looking at the brass bullet, Russell Conwell was impressed again that Johnny Ring's God had something greater for him to do.

His health recovered, he moved to Boston, where he wrote and lectured. The *Boston Traveler* and *New York Tribune* sent him to Europe where he interviewed Gladstone, Tennyson, Bismarck, and other greats.

But just as his influence was beginning to be felt worldwide, his wife died in 1872. The sorrow drove him to his knees and then back into a busy life where he vowed to work for eternal things.

He heard of a struggling Baptist church in Lexington, Massachusetts. "Yes, we would be proud to have you for our minister," the congregation said. So Russell Conwell began preaching from a regular pulpit. Soon the church was flourishing. Capacity crowds began attending. Then Conwell heard of another struggling church in Philadelphia.

He became pastor of the church when it was meeting in a tent. Within a few years, he led the Temple Baptist Church to build an auditorium seating four thousand.

He continued his outside lecturing with far-reaching results. In a lecture entitled "Perils of Democracy," he charged that colleges were developing an intellectual aristocracy and that high standards and expensive tuition were dooming poor youth to a life of ignorance. From this lecture came the great Temple University—now nineteenth largest in the nation—from which an estimated one hundred thousand people of all social classes passed during his lifetime.

Another lecture, "Acres of Diamonds"—his most famous—was delivered more than six thousand times in every corner of the globe. From the proceeds he helped educate ten thousand young men.

During his ministry he received into church membership more than six thousand previously non-Christians. Three giant hospitals were founded in relation to his church.

He wrote dozens of books, including the biographies of six Presidents. After his death, Russell Conwell was eulogized as the "penniless millionaire" for through his lectures and writings he had earned millions of dollars, but an accounting showed he had given most of it away.

When he was buried, the sword which Johnny Ring had given his life to rescue was placed in his hand. No one who knew Russell Conwell doubted that he had done the work of two men—and more.

Miracle in Hollywood

Charles E. Fuller

People at the wedding could not help but admire the young couple. Grace Payton was the beautiful daughter of the local country doctor. Charles Fuller was a successful orange grower and the superintendent of a great packing house in Southern California. At Pomona College he had received all highest scholastic honors and was captain of the football team.

"Charlie and Grace have so much to live for," someone whispered as the two swept down the church aisle after saying their marriage vows.

Charles and Grace Fuller had planned to have five or six children so they were delighted that Grace was expecting after a year of marriage. But to their sorrow the baby did not live.

Then Grace developed tuberculosis and had to spend most of the next three years in bed. She could not even attend church. That was no problem for Charles. Before Grace's illness, he had always found things to do on Sunday while she was in church. If there were no chores, then a nearby theater always offered a movie.

Grace was a Christian, having been led to Christ by a tubercular woman a few years earlier. Charles was not, but he was devoted to his beloved wife. He spent almost every spare moment at her bedside.

"Charlie, would you mind if I went with mother for a few weeks to Big Bear Lake?" she asked one morning. "The doctor thinks the change of climate might restore my health."

Devoted Charles Fuller smiled weakly. "I'll be terribly lonely, but if you think it will help, then go."

The days were lonely for Charlie after Grace left—especially the weekends. On Sundays he tried to occupy himself by reading the paper and polishing and fixing up his car. But the hours always seemed to drag by until it was time to go to the packing house on Monday morning.

One Saturday he read in an afternoon Los Angeles newspaper that a former amateur wrestler and boxer was to speak in the Church of the Open Door. The name, Paul Rader, sounded familiar. "Yes, that must be the same Paul Rader I knew in college," he said half aloud. "I'll go hear him preach."

When Charles Fuller entered the auditorium on the following Sunday afternoon he had difficulty finding a seat. Finally he settled for a place behind a pillar. Paul Rader, a nationally known evangelist, chose for his text Ephesians 1:18, "The eyes of your understanding being enlightened; that ye may know what is the hope of his calling, and what the riches of the glory of his inheritance in the saints."

The evangelist's words pierced Charles Fuller's heart. He leaned his head on the seat ahead of him and trembled, although at the time he did not know what was troubling him.

When the service was over, he hurried to his car.

He drove to a quiet spot on the edge of Franklin Park in Hollywood. He parked under a eucalyptus tree and climbed into the back seat, where he fell on his knees in prayer. That hour he surrendered his life to Christ.

Charles Fuller was then thirty years old. He was not aware that only a few blocks away was the Women's Club of Hollywood where he would one day begin a gospel radio program heard around the world.

Grace soon recovered from her illness. United now in Christ, the two plunged into active Christian work.

Mr. Fuller entered the ministry and served several years in a successful pastorate. In 1927 he attended a Bible conference in Indianapolis. Without previous warning he was asked to take the place of the regular speaker on a Christian radio program. After the program, an unusual number of letters were received telling of the blessing received.

While returning to California that same week, he was awakened from sleep by what he felt to be a message from God. "I want you to undertake a radio ministry for Me," the voice seemed to say.

For three hours Charles Fuller wrestled with the inner voice. At last he whispered, "Lord if Thou wilt go with me, I will do Your bidding."

In February 1928, Charles E. Fuller began broadcasting the gospel from Placentia, California on a single station. His radio ministry grew rapidly. By 1943, the Old Fashioned Revival Hour, with its familiar "Heavenly Sunshine" theme, was going forth over a thousand stations.

Today the Fullers are with the Lord, but they are remembered by millions—Charles for his preaching and Grace for her reading of letters from listeners. Mr.

Fuller has been credited with conducting the longest self-sustaining radio program of any kind in the history of broadcasting.

Billy Hits the Sawdust Trail

Billy Graham

The girls oohed and aahed at the young basketball and baseball star at Sharon High School near Charlotte, North Carolina. Someday he hoped to be a first baseman in the major leagues. If not that, he thought he might be a farmer like his father.

Billy was seventeen when an exprizefighter turned evangelist came to Charlotte. Mordecai Ham was an old-fashioned finger-pointing, fire-and-brimstone evangelist, who made a frontal assault upon sin.

Church leaders in Charlotte thought Mr. Ham a bit too much of a disturber. They refused him permission to erect a tent. But with laymen helping, the exboxer put down stakes just outside the city limits.

He had been holding meetings for several weeks when Billy came. Not that Billy—a tall, rangy boy with a mop of wavy blond hair—had been against going to church. He went every Sunday with his devout parents. And he neither smoked nor drank.

But there had been other things to do, and even though his father was a strong supporter of Mr. Ham, Billy just had not taken the trouble to attend before.

The crowd was big for Charlotte—five thousand people. People were saying that it was the biggest thing ever to hit the Carolinas. Billy and his high school friends walked down the sawdust aisles and took their seats on a hard bench.

The sermon from the big preacher was quite unimpressive to Billy. That is until the preacher jabbed a pointed finger in Billy's direction, and shouted, "You're a sinner."

Billy—who was not one to duck a fast ball—was not ready to play catch with the preacher. He ducked his blond head behind the hat of a woman in front of him.

Two nights later Billy went back, taking a friend, Albert McMakin, along with him. For several nights afterward the two attended together. The fiery evangelist kept hammering away, driving home to Billy that he had to make a choice between heaven or hell.

One night Billy took another friend, Grady Wilson. "Let's sit in the choir," Billy suggested, although he knew he could not carry a tune in a basket. So the two sat behind the pulpit, safely out of the gaze of the pulpit-thumping preacher.

Mordecai Ham did not point his finger at Billy that night, but Billy got the impact of his message when he said, "There's a great sinner here tonight."

He's talking about me, Billy thought. *Someone must have told him I was here.*

The preacher concluded his sermon and gave the call for penitents to hit the sawdust trail. Billy was gulping hard when the choir began singing. After a brief burst of song he could stand it no longer. "Come on, Grady," he told his companion.

The two picked their way down from the choir and stood at the front.

Recalling his decision, Billy said, "It was like being

141

outdoors on a dark day and having the sun burst through the cloud cover. Everything looked different. I knew for the first time the joy of being born again."

Since that memorable night in 1936, Billy Graham has already preached to more people than the late Reverend Mordecai Ham, the man who led him to Christ. In fact he has preached to more, face to face—over twenty million—than any preacher in history. But even more important, he has seen tens of thousands walk the sawdust trail and come into the prayer room to find Christ.

A Father's Legacies

William Cameron Townsend

The dry desert wind whirled a curtain of choking dust around the vegetable cart. The little man with a long beard spurred his horse on. Beside him trotted his eight-year-old son, Cameron.

They turned into cobblestoned Telegraph Avenue, a main street of Los Angeles in the year 1902. A block ahead, the farmer reined in his horse beside a grocery and went inside. "What do you have today, Will?" the burly Italian asked. The farmer listed his products for sale and added a description of their size and condition. The groceryman added up the totals of what he wanted and handed the farmer his money.

While Will Townsend unloaded the order, young Cameron stood eyeing the groceryman. "You don't check what my pa tells you. He could sell you anything."

The Italian grinned. "He could, little man. But he wouldn't. Along the avenue here we call your pa the honest deaf man. His word is as good as gold."

Late that afternoon, father and son arrived home. Molly Townsend had supper ready. It was not much, just vegetables and water, but they bowed their heads while deaf Will prayed. Cam noticed that he always ended, "May the knowledge of the Lord cover the earth as the waters cover the sea."

The Townsends were poor—dirt poor. Will tried to scrape a living from tenant farming, but there was hardly ever enough to feed his growing family of four daughters and two sons. When Cameron's little brother Paul was born, there was only thirty-five cents in the house. One year times were so bad that two of the girls had to be cared for by relatives.

But they were not complainers. "The Lord gives and the Lord takes away," Will would say. "Maybe we'll do better next year."

Good times or bad, Cam noticed that his deaf father read three chapters of the Bible each day of the week and five every Sunday. After breakfast came family Bible reading, a hymn, and prayers. His deafness, caused by a blow from a tipped plank back in Kansas, didn't keep Will from singing. When his voice rose higher than the ceiling and cracked, the children were under strict orders from Molly not to laugh.

While Will still had a little hearing, the children recited the books of the Bible, the Ten Commandments, and other selected passages into his left ear. When he became completely deaf, they wrote out their memory work for his approval.

Molly and the children always attended Presbyterian services. Will went until he could no longer hear. Then he usually stayed home, read sermons from the *Christian Herald,* and cooked dinner. If there was a visiting preacher, Molly often brought him home.

Cameron could not remember a time when he did not believe. After his pet rabbit died, he prayed for it to be raised from the dead. He decided that if the Lord should answer his prayer, the rabbit would be uncomfortable in its grave. So in the darkness of night he tiptoed out of the house and dug up the rabbit.

At twelve Cameron asked for membership in the church. Afterward Will took him into the barn and questioned his beliefs. Satisfied, he recommended that the boy be accepted.

Professions of faith by the other children were just as nondramatic. But their faith was strong, and they adopted the Christian virtues of their parents.

When Cameron was ready for Occidental College, Will found a farm near the campus and an older daughter postponed her marriage a year to work and help pay his tuition. When Cameron volunteered to go to Guatemala as a Bible salesman at only twenty-one, the family gave him their blessing and sent money from time to time. When he finished translating the New Testament for the Cakchiquel Indians of Guatemala— a ten-year task, Will and Molly wrote the last two words into the manuscript. By this time their youngest son was a missionary too. Molly died a few months later, but Will lived on and helped Cameron operate the first school for Bible translators in America. He was the school cook.

During the next five years, deaf Will prayed and helped his son enlist Bible translators for Mexico's Indians. On Christmas Eve, 1939, Cameron received word that his father was dead. At the time he did not have the funds to travel to the funeral.

In writing his sisters and brothers, he listed some legacies from his father. He put at the top:

His faithfulness in pointing me to God and
His Word

His habit of telling the truth at all costs

Cameron Townsend moved on to establish the Wycliffe Bible Translators, now over twenty-five hundred strong, and translating Scripture into over five hundred languages in twenty-three countries. At seventy-six, his memory of his father remains clear.

"He and mother never had much in this world," he recalls. "But they led each of their children to trust in Christ and to love the Bible."

A Ring and a Prayer

Vonette Bright

The trim brunette's eyes flashed as she said good-bye to her closest friend. "Either Bill will give up this fanaticism or I will come back without a ring. Wish me luck."

With that, the trim young woman was off to Los Angeles for a showdown with her fiancé.

Vonette Zachary and Bill Bright had known each other since their elementary school days in Oklahoma. A small girl with an iron will, Vonette had admired Bill as an outstanding student and a gifted debater. She thought him so brilliant that he could one day be President and hoped that the man she married might be as outstanding.

Bill went on to college. By the time Vonette was a freshman at Texas State College for Women, he had graduated and was in business. She thought of him occasionally, but in no special way.

At the time she was wrestling with doubts about childhood beliefs. She had been active in church during high school, but now attendance at church services seemed meaningless.

The summer following her first year, an unexpected letter came from Bill. The letterhead proclaiming "Bright's California Confections" looked impressive.

147

He wrote about visiting the Coconut Grove and seeing a film star who reminded him of Vonette. He wished her a nice summer and said he would be thinking of her.

Vonette showed the letter to her father, who said, "Well, he's made good, and now he'll be coming home for his bride." The remark piqued her pride, and she decided to ignore the letter.

But back in college that fall, she came across the letter in a desk drawer and mentioned it to her room-mate. "He sounds too good to pass up," her roommate advised. "Better write him."

She wrote ten pages that night.

That started the romance. Air mail special delivery letters began arriving, then flowers, candy, telegrams, telephone calls. Vonette's debonair and charming boyfriend became the talk of the campus. Even before Bill visited the campus the following March, she was ready to say yes.

They were engaged for the rest of her time in college. However, her happiness was clouded by Bill's fervent religious faith. He suggested passages of Scripture for her to read and presented requests for prayer. Vonette finally concluded that her businessman beau was a religious fanatic who needed cooling off.

In turn, Bill began to suspect that Vonette was not really a Christian. He loved her, yet he felt they should not marry unless she changed. Shortly before her scheduled graduation, he invited her to California for a college conference.

She came equally determined that Bill must change or else.

The conference was held at Forest Home, a Christian

retreat center in California. Here she met attractive, dynamic young people who were just as strong in their beliefs as Bill. Despite her prejudices, she had to admire them for the happiness and purpose in life they seemed to share.

One evening when she and Bill were discussing what made these friends so different from other young adults, she realized that their beliefs were right for them and him. Religion had not helped her, so she felt it best to slip out of Bill's life. At the end of the week she would give back the ring and return home.

"I'd like you to talk to Henrietta Mears," he said. "She has helped more young people than anybody I know."

Vonette could not see any harm in this, so she agreed.

The remarkable Christian educator who had built a Sunday school to six thousand members in Hollywood showed Vonette from the Bible how to know God for certain. She described the plan and purpose which God had for Vonette's life. She helped Vonette see that all had sinned and fallen short of God's perfection. Vonette had desperately tried to be good, and had even kept lists of areas in her life to be improved. Miss Mears explained that Christ had died for her sins and offered the gift of eternal life if she would accept it.

Finally Vonette bowed her head and asked Christ to come into her life. At the time, she saw herself standing in darkness on the edge of a diving board and jumping into the unknown. The image was striking because she could not swim.

She discovered the secret of the joy in the lives of her fiancé and the other young people. The Bible became her guide, and day by day she became more aware of Christ's living presence in her life.

Bill and Vonette began the great adventure of life together on December 30, 1948. Bill felt God wanted him in a special ministry, so he enrolled in nearby Fuller Seminary. Three years later, he and Vonette felt drawn toward student work, and they moved near the campus of the University of California at Los Angeles (UCLA).

Bill recruited a gospel team to visit the fraternities, sororities, and other student groups at UCLA. That first year they saw about two hundred and fifty students become Christians. By the following year five young men had joined the staff of the newly established Campus Crusade for Christ.

In the years since, Campus Crusade under the leadership of Bill Bright has expanded to blanket the free world. It was perhaps the major catalyst to the Jesus Movement of the late sixties and early seventies. No other evangelistic movement in modern times has equaled its outreach.

The Brights live frugally on missionary salaries. Their deepening love for each other is obvious to the thousands of students who visit Crusade headquarters at Arrowhead Springs, California. When Vonette speaks, she usually relates their courtship experiences. "I'm grateful for a husband who walks close to God," she says. "When I don't agree with him, I pray, 'Lord give me the heart to respond.' God has given Bill the vision to lead and me the heart to follow."

The Gang Leader's Last Rumble

Tom Skinner

He was a black preacher's kid in the Harlem ghetto,
a rectangle two-and-one-half miles long and a mile
wide, into which were crammed over a million poor
people. His playground was a vacant lot with shattered bottles, rusty cans, and an abandoned car. He
knew about the rats that gnawed on black babies in
rundown tenements where people paid outrageous rents
to absentee landlords. He saw racketeers paying off the
police. He was aware of the hordes of welfare children growing up without fathers. Drugs, gambling, ex-
tortion, rape, murder, sex crimes, robbery, stench, and
ever-present poverty were the everyday sights, sounds,
and smells of his growing up.

Tom Skinner joined the church at seven and was as
faithful as the church mouse. After a while he began
to choke on the emotional laundromat that passed for
worship. He got to where he could predict every word
and motion of the pastor, people, and choir. He discovered the two-facedness of many church members
and ministers. He heard preachers bragging about
their women and the amount received in the offerings.

He grew resentful and rebellious.

The black nationalists began explaining Christianity
to Tom as they saw it. "The white man uses it to keep

Negroes in their place," they said. They inferred that any right-thinking black would reject Christianity as "neocolonialist" and "out of date" and get the "honkies" off his neck. White Christians, they argued, preached to blacks about love, while denying them the right to fair employment and escape from the ghetto.

At the peak of his resentment, Tom was invited to join the gang called the Harlem Lords and take the initiation test.

They tied his hands in front and hung him from a giant spike. After ripping off his shirt, a tall gang member lashed him with a leather whip until he was almost unconscious. Because he took the beating without crying out, Tom was made a member.

After six weeks of fighting with other gangs and petty stealing, he challenged the head of the Lords to a knife duel. They squared off in a garbage-strewn alley, and after several feints and thrusts, Tom slipped a knife into his opponent's side.

For the next two years he reigned as undisputed leader of one of the most feared gangs in New York City. He led them in fifteen big rumbles, and they never lost. They were under his absolute control. If he told one to go home and steal from his mother, he would do it.

Tom's hatred for whites increased until he could not stand to be near someone of another race. He blamed whites for every problem of blacks. He took out his frustration against the dominant society by stealing and destroying property.

At church he played the role of a model boy. He memorized verses with the rest of the young people and recited the clichés his folks wanted to hear. Behind the masquerade he felt pity and disgust for the church people.

The chance came for the Lords to become the most powerful gang in Harlem—if they could help win the biggest gang war of Tom's career.

The rumble would pit five gangs—the Lords, the Imperials, the Crowns, the Sportsmen, and the Jesters —against an alliance of gangs from the other side of the city. Over three thousand young toughs would be involved. And Tom was assigned to plan strategy for his side.

He sat mulling over his plans while half listening to his favorite disc jockey spin rock-and-roll records in the background. There was a station break at nine o'clock, and to his dismay a gospel program came on. He swore softly and banged his fist.

An honor student in school, Tom noticed that the radio preacher had atrocious grammer. He was also emotional, an approach to religion Tom despised. He thought of changing stations, but somehow felt compelled to listen.

The uneducated preacher quoted 2 Corinthians 5: 17: "Therefore if any man be in Christ, he is a new creature: old things are passed away; behold, all things are become new."

Tom had heard the Scripture a hundred times. But he had never been so impressed as the preacher hurled a challenge. "It doesn't matter who you are or what you have done," he said. "Christ came to earth to change your sinful nature. He is your answer. He can straighten out the mess you've made of your life. He will change that 'factory' inside that makes you sin."

As the man preached, Tom argued back in his mind,

recalling all the reasons he knew for rejecting Christianity. The Holy Spirit demolished them one by one, and before the program ended, the young gang leader had to admit that he was a phony who had never put God to the test.

He bowed his head and prayed simply. "Lord, I don't understand all about You and the Bible. But if what this preacher says is true, forgive my sins and change my life."

No lights flashed, no thunder roared; he simply accepted God's promises as given and became a new man.

The acid test came when he faced one hundred twenty-nine Harlem Lords and told them what had happened. He fully expected Mop, the number two man in the gang, so named because of his practice of mopping up blood with his foot, to put a knife in his ribs. But no one raised a hand against him.

Two nights later he saw Mop on the street. "I was gonna really cut you up, Tom," he said. "But Somebody held me back."

Mop was Tom Skinner's first convert, but certainly not his last. After winning several other gang members to Christ, Tom became a noted evangelist and is today the foremost speaker for young black evangelicals.

Militant for Christ, he has attracted support from a wide spectrum of church leaders, both black and white.

Billy Graham believes "God has a unique work" for him. Congressman John B. Anderson, a white moderate, thinks, "Some may be upset by his portrayal of Christ as a revolutionary. Those who really ponder his message," the Congressman adds, "will see that there is no gap between New Testament Christianity and a genuine solution to some of the most vexing problems of our times."

Melvin Banks, a black publisher of Sunday school curriculum, declares: "Tom insists that Christ invades the racial turmoil not to 'take sides' but to 'take charge.' "

"Lift-Off" for the Space Scientist

Werner von Braun

Werner von Braun was weary of the world as he walked along the desert road near the US Army missile testing site at White Sands, New Mexico. World War II was over. Dr. von Braun and his team of German rocket experts had chosen to surrender to the Allies instead of the Russians. After working under Hitler, he had no desire to help another dictator, Stalin. Never having wanted to use his skills for warfare, the world's greatest rocket expert hoped now to be a part of a peaceful space venture.

An old bus lumbered by and stopped at a house up ahead. Von Braun noticed the name Church of the Nazarene, El Paso on the side. Investigating, he found that the pastor drove the old bus fifty miles every Sunday to pick up people for worship in a wooden barracks.

Sunday after Sunday, von Braun watched the bus come by the missile site. It brought back memories of his Lutheran childhood in Germany when his faith had been simple but real. During his years of scientific study and work, he had drifted away. Now he knew that there had to be higher values than science if man were to survive on earth.

Aware of an aching spiritual void, he read the Fulton Oursler books and Hurlbut's *Story of the Bible*. Then he moved into serious Bible study. "The truth of Christ emerged like a revelation," he recalls. "I realized I had been a Christian in name only."

He moved his family to Huntsville, Alabama, where he was named director of the George C. Marshall Space Flight Center. They joined the local Episcopal Church of the Nativity. As the space program accelerated to the point where powerful rockets, designed and built by the von Braun team began sending men to the moon, his personal faith grew.

A natural headliner because of his leadership in the space program, Von Braun received more invitations to speak and write than he could handle. For those assignments he could accept, he gave priority to spiritual views.

For example, he spoke at the Colorado governor's prayer breakfast in Denver on the subject "A Scientist's Belief in God." "The public has a deep respect for the amazing scientific advances made within our lifetime," the high-cheekboned, blond space expert said. "There is admiration for the scientific process of observation, experimentation, of testing every concept to measure its validity. But it still bothers some people that we cannot prove scientifically that God exists. Must we light a candle to see the sun?"

"Many who believe in God as Creator," he added, "have difficulty accepting Him as a personal God who is interested, not only in the human race, but in the individual. Many modern theologians . . . emphasize the 'group' or all mankind, rather than the individual, and symbols of reality."

157

After noting that "man can know God only by His self-revelation in the person of Jesus Christ, as witnessed by Scripture," he declared, "In our search to know God . . . Jesus Christ should be the focus of our efforts, and our inspiration."

Dozens of speeches later, when Apollo 9 was on the launch pad and primed for blast-off into moon orbit, Von Braun gave a long statement of his theological views to *Miami Herald* reporter Adon C. Taft.

"I am certain there are other beings in the universe." He mused that Christ's sacrifice on earth might be sufficient for the other beings in the universe. Just because the crucifixion occurred on earth, he suggested, "does not limit His validity for a greater environment."

Von Braun expressed his belief in a final judgment and "the immortality of the soul which can cherish the reward or suffer the penalty decreed." He saw a scientific foundation for "the continuity of our spiritual existence," and added, "Science has found that nothing can disappear without a trace. Nature does not know extinction. All it knows is transformation. Now, if God applies this fundamental principle to the most minute and insignificant parts of His universe, doesn't it make sense to assume that He applies it also to the masterpiece of His creation—the human soul? I think it does."

Now promoted to be deputy director of the National Aeronautics and Space Administration, the world's best-known space scientist looks forward to landings on Mars and other planets. But he is also concerned about the advance of Christianity. "When mankind was given the opportunity to know Christ almost two thousand years ago," he notes, "the world was turned upside down through the widespread witness of His followers. The same thing could happen today."

Index